My Agape

A MEMOIR

My Agape

A MEMOIR

WWW.13THANDJOAN.COM

13th & Joan books may be purchased for educational, business or sales promotional use. For information, please email the Sales Department at sales@13thandjoan.com.

Printed in the U.S.A.

First Printing, June 2018

Library of Congress Cataloging-in-Publication Data has been applied for.

ISBN 978-1-7335154-4-3

agape

early 17th century: from Greek agapē 'selfless love.'

1. *adj*
with the mouth wide open as in wonder or awe

2. *noun*
selfless love of one person for another without sexual
implications (especially love that is spiritual in nature)

Dedication

This story is dedicated to Jewel Jefferson Dozier; and to all of my students who showed up early to class, stayed late after class, ate lunch with me, or even just randomly stopped by just to vent about their life experiences.

These are my experiences & my true uncandid responses to LIFE.

I AM SHE & SHE IS ME.

This is proof that nothing can stop your reign, Queen.

Foreword

Struggle: *noun*
1. a forceful or violent effort to get free of restraint or resist attack.
"a power struggle for the leadership"
synonyms: fight, scuffle, brawl, tussle, wrestling bout, skirmish, fracas, melee;
conflict, contest, battle, confrontation, clash, skirmish

Resilient: *adjective*
1. (of a person or animal) able to withstand or recover quickly from difficult conditions.
"babies are generally far more resilient than new parents realize"
synonyms: strong, tough, hardy

Perseverance: *noun*
1. steadfastness in doing something despite difficulty or delay in achieving success.
"his perseverance with the technique illustrates his single-mindedness"
synonyms: persistence, tenacity, determination, staying power, indefatigability, steadfastness, purposefulness

Achievement: *noun*
1. a thing done successfully, typically by effort, courage, or skill.
"to reach this stage is a great achievement"
synonyms: attainment, realization, accomplishment, fulfillment, implementation, execution, performance
2. the process or fact of achieving something.
"the achievement of professional recognition"

Hope: *noun*

noun: hope; *plural noun:* hopes

1. a feeling of expectation and desire for a certain thing to happen.

"he looked through her belongings in the hope of coming across some information"

synonyms: aspiration, desire, wish, expectation, ambition, aim, goal, plan, design

These five words definitively describe Shawna Brooks. As a child, she came into my life with a struggle. Because of her resilience, she graduated from high school with honors and, then, accepted the role as a mother figure to her younger sister after losing her own mother. That same resilience enabled her to obtain a Bachelor's of Science Degree from Bethune Cookman University and her Master's of Teaching Degree from Georgia State University . As the reader, it is my strong desire that you will get hope from her story as she has given me hope from knowing her.

Steven Campbell

What can I say about her? I'm proud to say that I know Shawna Brooks. I watched her grow into the productive, strong woman that she is today. I was her mother's best friend. That was my sister for life and when Shawna was a child, she was always unique. While demonstrating leadership and integrity, Shawna knew the difference between right and wrong, and at a very young age, could identify when something needed to be changed. Being a mom is a great responsibility and she knew the job was going to be one of the biggest challenges of her life. This took a lot of patience and even more love. A next level type of love. As women, life always has its challenges and sometimes, we don't see it coming. We don't always get the effort back that we put into life. Life shows up and shows out, but this story is proof that life's tallest, biggest, baddest, mountains can be angelically life changing. I have seen every card that life has dealt and this is what separates Shawna Brooks and makes her special . I know that there's more for her to finish in this life, but this is her time to share that incredible, unconditional love with the world. I believe that Shawna's ambition and "Love of Life and Humanity" will continue to motivate and inspire many to do wonderful things.

I am very honored to say that I know & love Shawna Brooks.

Kennia Elizabeth Sanchez
AKA "The Darkistofq"
"Queenie"

Preface

As I sit here looking at my class, I fight through the everyday struggle to just write. I'm broke as hell and paying for bills, and life is challenging as well. My emotions are on high, and this is truly the hardest thing I've ever done in my life. I feel a "gut punch" everytime I finish a chapter. I hold back tears as I re-read and re-live at the same time. It's torture and freedom all in the same thought. I wanted to write this book so badly because I know that God really wants me to share this testimony, because it glorifies just how powerful He is. God has been preparing me to share this with you for quite some time. My doubt and anxiety come from so many angles, but yet, God is steady pushing for me to be the light for someone who needs it. I'm surprised that I have made this much progress in a short amount of time. The universe has been persistent on me telling this story for some time now. Every time I begin to tell others about my life, they look at me in total astonishment. I'm often told that I have a hell of a story to share. It took me three years to really get serious about writing this book. Honestly, it wasn't until I started my job that I am at, writing, right now, that I became serious about telling my story. As I write, one girl, in particular, surfaces in my thoughts. She was in my third period Biology class, and she reminded me of myself. She was a smart girl who was just pushing to beat the odds. She was beautiful and popular, too. She was social with everyone, and cordial, even if she didn't like you. She would often come and sit by my desk and complete her work so she could immediately turn it in to avoid her peers from copying her work. We often spoke about the books she was reading along with my life and dreams outside of teaching. She knew how much I wanted to write a book. Immediately, she was interested in reading it as she expressed that her favorite genre

was always a good memoir. I ensured her that my life was similar to those gritty tell-all success stories. She was always reading a book or telling me about a book when I saw her, and she was going to be one of my first readers. I enjoyed our teacher-student relationship. We met in August of 2017, but she died, tragically, in October 2017. She was shot in the face by her boyfriend; and she died in her bedroom. Her death made the six o'clock news; and the news spread through our small, school community like wildfire. I tried not to react in front of the students, but I was shaken to my core by this violent act that had taken the life of one of my favorite students. I was genuinely sad; I found myself having to go into the bathroom to cry. She was me. She had the potential to be far greater than she ever imagined, but she was just looking for love in all the wrong places. Her name was Jewel, and she needed to hear my story, like so many others, to bear witness that success is not bias. Jewel was a born winner, like me; but she was young and hadn't begun to realize her gifts, talents, and greatness. Jewel's death moved me to get serious about sharing my story to bear witness to whoever needs it. To just know that it's ok to be different from your friends, it's cool to be brilliant, and love will come. You can truly do anything that your heart desires, and the possibilities are limitless.

The world, and the unworldly people in it, often bring about the extreme experiences into our life. I think the unfortunate reality is that life is extreme; and people crack. There's no real manual on how to deal with the crazy in life. Many good people don't make it past the crazy, because life comes at you fast, and sometimes, even knocks you down. I think it is my civic duty to share with you that life WILL definitely knock you down, but every time you get up, you're better and stronger. I want every individual to know that as long as you believe you can, you will. Crazy circumstances don't make you crazy; but they will make your faith and your grind insane. My dear student didn't make it past her extremes in life, but if she was still here, these are some of the things I would share about fighting the good fight in life and making it out on top.

Acknowledgements

I can't begin to thank anyone without first thanking God. It wasn't until I truly found my peace with Him, that I was able to really sit down and share my story, along with His glory. I am beyond thankful for the key players He has placed in my life since birth. It's almost like He built an entire football team just for me. From family and friends to coworkers and strangers—I value every individual beyond words; and I appreciate what each person has deposited into my life. My starting line up has lasted the test of time, and this is all happening because of you.

To my sister, Rashieta—I am forever grateful for your friendship, tough love, protection, and lessons on not being swallowed up by this cold world. I owe my drive and my grind to you.

To my Uncle Butch, and both of my heavenly angels, Elouise Tribue and Andrena Brooks—I feel your love deep in my veins; and I know I owe my earthly grace to you.

To Steven—I am forever grateful for you sticking with the kid! I appreciate you being my father, my mentor, my accountability partner, and my therapist all at the same time, whenever I need any or all of the above. Thank you for helping me change my family legacy to greatness, and nothing less.

To Shaquana, my sister—The amount of unconditional love you bring into my life is so essential and impactful on me. Outside of the fact that you are completely clutch in my life at any given time, you inspire me to be kind always, and I admire that.

To Kameesha, my BFF—I am forever grateful for the balance you have brought into my life, and for you taking the time to not only

know me, but understand me; and for really teaching me how to nurture my sister as a parent, and knowing when not to stress. Looking at the brighter side of things has been a process for me, but I owe so many of my strides to you. I can genuinely say I am less of a "worry-bug" because of our "fuck-it" conversations. I feel like I have gotten closer to God because you remind me so often how blessed I really am, and how far I have come.

To Imani, my friend that has always been more like family—You are my inspiration to go hard and be gracious, because you always go so hard for me and would give your last without blinking. Your whole family is my family, and I love y'all for the love and support you've shown me.

To Ms. Anquinette Jones—I know you pray for me, lady, and I love you forever for that!!! I appreciate you being my angel at work and teaching me how to teach effectively, pray effectively, and be strong in faith.

To all my friends, who support me in EVERYTHING (I'm sorry I can't name you all, but 1305 Grant Projects, NSHS & BCU squad all day), I love you and my gratitude is far beyond words!

To the friends of friends and strangers that have walked into my life and blessed it physically or figuratively, I greatly appreciate you.

And, last, but far from least, Lyniah Skye Brooks. You are the golden child. You have brought the light into my life and ARE the reason for the season! I love you for loving me so much, and loving me THROUGH so much; flaws and all. On my darkest days, you are just so bright; and I am immensely proud to say that you are going to be so much better than me.

Introduction

Some might say that I am Hell on a Scale. This is definitely a figure of speech that describes what I've encountered. The phrase also represents the fact that the series of events in my life could have been worse on a scale of comparison to others. My experiences have influenced my perception over time, and morphed an individual who is going to give you hell about what I want and what I think.

When I wake up, my battle with my emotions begin. I pray on my way in and on my way out—of sleep, that is. I'm handling life, but it's difficult. I'm emotional, but I've mastered the skill of masking my feelings. I don't have feelings. It's almost like tunnel vision, because I try so hard not to focus on my feelings. Most of the time, I feel like an emotional mess. So, I put on that, "I don't have feelings" front. It makes it hard to date or even pursue anyone, but I've slowly accepted the isolation in this process. Writing and sharing this story has been one of the hardest journeys yet; and you will soon know I have had a few journeys. I prayed daily on my biggest hurdle at this time in my life, which is loneliness. Many days I'm sad and I can't help it. I want to feel love, I want someone to love me and care for me. Of course, I know my friends, family, and even strangers love me, but it's not the same. Not like someone really loving you. Like REAL love. When nothing was genuine and everything seemed empty, I prayed for God to fill me with His spirit and take away my lonely feelings. I wasn't depressed, but it was a different type of low. Lows that were too transparent for my spirit child. I was struggling with everything around me, mentally and spiritually. It's ten times worse when your friends and family look at you and they can't find the thought to understand what's wrong. They feel you are on top of everything, and you're doing great.

People will see you and think, "They've got it all figured out," and you're literally bleeding on the inside. THAT WAS MY FIGHT. My opponent was how I looked on the outside versus how I felt everyday. Being emotionally broken is not something that I am proud of, but it does speak to how I react to life .

As you turn the pages of this journey, I don't want you to feel any emotion towards me. I want you to think about everything that makes you want to quit, and fight harder. As a fighter, I also want you to know and recognize grace. Nothing can overpower love, which brings about grace. The amount of love that God has for you, the amount of love in this world for you, and the amount of self-love that you have for yourself can be groundbreaking. This is a story of "the tearing down and building up' of just that. In the presence of such a power, great things manifest. Diamonds do form under great pressure and fill the path to greatness. Each experience will drop a jewel in your life—good, bad, or indifferent. This journey has allowed me to appreciate every gem on top of the dirt and flourish in self-love. A love like no other, no regret, no shame; just love. I want you to feel as free as I do, and then, fly high with it. The sky's the limit. Be limitless on the way to greatness.

—*Love*

Table of Contents

Meet The OG's

Harlem 1989

It was a hot summer day in New York City, and my mother, Dreanie and her best friend, Kenya, were out hiking it up the block to the Rastas' trap to get a blunt. The Rastas had their own lil' apartment in Harlem where they trapped and smoked. My mother's friend, Kenya, started talking to the guy she was buying from, and he invited them in to smoke. My mom accompanied her, as a good friend would, and he had a friend sitting down on the couch inside. So, my mom started talking to the friend, and Kenya was across the room talking to her friend. Out of the blue, my mother gets up and storms across the room. "We gotta go now!" she said. "This nigga's done lost his mind...and he's stupid."

"Whoa! What happened?" Kenya replied. "We're just chilling; and we just got here. What's he doing?"

The guy Kenya was talking to stepped in and said, "It's okay. He's no harm. I'm 'bout to roll up again."

So, my mother goes back over to sit with the friend again, and he repeats his question to her. "You wanna fuck?" he asked. That was it! My mother was mad; and she got up and was ready to walk out. Kenya got her friend's number, and they left quickly.

Kenya had been talking to her Rasta friend on the phone since that day, and he invited them back over. My mother was not with it, but Kenya insisted she be a good friend by accompanying her again; and if nothing else, to just come smoke. So, they went back to the trap, and of course, the rude rasta friend was there. My mom walked in with an attitude. The Rasta friend asked, "Why she mad?" in his deep, island accent.

"Why were you coming at me like that last time?" my mother asked. He simply replied, "I thought that's what you American girls like." My mother looked at him in astonishment because, one, she thought he couldn't speak much English; and, two, what

American girl did that work on? He went on to explain how he was from Belize, and that was what he's always been told about American girls. My mother went off and let him know that he definitely had the wrong American girl; and not to ever try that again. Then, they smoked and laughed about it. They became inseparable after that. He was in love with everything about my mother; and soon came me.

Meet Baby G

The air outside cut like knives. The streets were busy, and the sidewalks were covered with ice and moving legs scurrying to get out the way. Cabs cutting everyday drivers off, and horns blaring through the window. January 19,1990 in St. Luke Roosevelt Hospital maternity unit, Shawna Fatima Brooks was born...8lbs and 9oz. On the opposite end of the spectrum, my older sister's father died of pneumonia in his sleep on January 19, 1990. It was a very bittersweet day for our household; and it was hard for everyone to be happy about a baby.

I was a brown, round, and chunky baby, with a head full of hair. My father and mother highly anticipated my arrival because my father really loved my mother, and it was her time to do it all over with him. Well, have a child, that is. I was welcomed into the crisp cool air of Harlem, New York. That soon fell to shit very quickly. My father was a native of Belize and my mother was Philly born and Harlem raised. My mother was 22 years old; and her heart was ride or die. No job, no desire to work; and her only motive was get money. Her heart was saddened over the lost of her first love so suddenly. Yet, she was still overjoyed with her new baby girl; and my father made life comfortable for her. My mother was advisor #1 to my father, who was rasta to the core, and a hustler to the death of him. He was a very smart man, and analytical about everything. Literally, one of the most successful drug dealers in Harlem, but (and there's always a but) money breeds envy. Just like a snapshot in memory, he was gone. Nine months after my birth my father was murdered.

I remember so vividly my mother telling me how much my father wanted a daughter, but I also remember the tragic events that she said led up to his death. There was a rat in his inner circle, and they hated that "the foreigner" ran Harlem. My father sold drugs all throughout Harlem, and had several houses full of drugs and money throughout New York City. He was in his prime when he met my mother; and my mother appreciated the peace of mind after the death of my sister's father. My mother said my dad's initial plan was for me to be born in Belize; however, I was born in New York on the account of my mother's poor planning and my stubbornness, which soon made it impossible for her to fly.

Shortly after I was born, the first attempt to bring down my father happened at his main money house in uptown Harlem. He was supposed to be there taking inventory of the drugs and counting money how he usually did, but my mother had him making baby runs in Harlem. My mother's tedious tasks saved his life that day. The house was raided by dozens of cops and all the drugs and money was seized by NYPD. That was a record loss. My father switched up his routine and his second house still got shot up by the forever anonymous about a month later. God was on his side only because he wasn't in place this day either, thanks to my mother. My mother soon felt the heat, and was a little nervous after the past few attempts on my father's life and livelihood. She applied for my passport to go to Belize. During this time, my father had traveled back to Belize to handle some work with his business partner; and unfortunately never made it back to Harlem. My father never crossed state lines again. His body was found washed up on the shores of Mexico about a week later. Friends wanted to say he drowned, but my father swam in the ocean everyday. The family will always believe my father was murdered; and he was. The devils that secretly wished him death were victorious. I never got the chance to form any memories with my father; he is just a story that was occasionally told to me. From what I hear, my father was book smart just as much as he was street smart, and was an over-thinker, just like me. He was finished with high school when he was 16 years old in Belize, and could have been anything in the world; but he went with the fast money, which was what he was good at. The fast money cost him his life.

My mother and I, who was now 10 months old at the time, boarded the plane to Belize to bury my father; and wound up staying a few months because she was sad over a love lost twice in less than a year. She was 23 years old, with two kids by two different men, who were both dead. I think that is when my mother officially lost herself, and never truly returned. I think she stuck around for the comfort; and for the help with her new baby girl. Everyone knew and loved my mom, Dreanie, so it was all love.

We stayed in Belize until I was almost two. My grandmother cared for me while my mother tried to find her mind. I was an island baby living an island life, dreads and all. I was christened in Belize at this huge church, and the festivities lasted three days. My family, and the people of Belize City, mourned my father by loving on me. Everyone came to know "Derek's Daughter," and it made them proud.

My mother eventually left Belize to get back to my older sister in New York, who was staying with her grandmother. My mother grieved in her own way, but unfortunately, life went on, and she had two kids with no job and no man. It was the vicious cycle of events; and all my mother knew was "get up and make it happen." My mother got back to New York and made sure my sister, Rashieta, and everything else was copacetic. She, then, went uptown to check on her mother and siblings. After home was secured, my mom had to meet up with her girls and get her head together. She had the space and opportunity to move and shake as she needed. Time moved swiftly while I stayed in Belize. By the time my mother made it back to truly decide that I wasn't going to be raised in Belize by my grandmother, I had dreads, and I was walking. My mother snapped out of her depression right after I turned two; or should I say, pulled it together momentarily, because I was on a plane back to New York before the city got hot for the summer.

New York was blazing hot and I had dreads. Ugly, nappy, big, dreads; and my mother hated them. From what I was told, her first order of business was to cut my hair. Let her tell it, I was hideous; and I didn't look like a girl. My mother wasn't with it; and she cut my hair into a baby fro. Her baby was not about to walk around with messy dreads. My mother was happy to bring her chubby, light skin baby home, but I always tend to wonder who I would be if I was raised in Belize.

Harlem, New York 1995

So the summer breeze passed swiftly as my thick, nappy hair grew back. I remember being young, on the train, back and forth between where my sister lived with her grandmother (her father's mother) and my nana's house which was my mother's mother. My sister and I saw each other often, but when my mother had to go, we went to separate houses. My sister was very sickly during this time; having back to back surgeries on her leg. My mom had always believed that the staff at Harlem Hospital had dropped my sister when she was born and injured her leg. The doctors called it something fancy in medical terms. They explained to my mom that one leg was growing faster than the other, and they needed to do surgery to stop growth in one leg and allow it time to catch up. It took my sister longer to walk; and then she had to learn to walk all over again. This would be the culprit behind my sister's limp in the years to come.

Needless to say, my mother stayed gone, in the hospital with my sister, and I was uptown in Frederick Douglass Housing Projects with my nana, aunt, and two uncles. For the lack of better terms, my mom was all over the place, but she made it work. When my sister was well, we were in the streets, back and forth between the Bronx and Harlem. My mother's apartment was in the Bronx and my nana lived in Harlem. When my mom wasn't out and didn't need a babysitter or my nana was too drunk, we took the BX15 to the last stop in the Bronx. They were sometimes the longest, coldest rides, too; however, my mom would get us in the house and cook, no matter how late it was. She cooked in sections, so it took forever, but it was always good. My mother was under a lot of pressure at that time. I think between my sister being in and out of surgery and rehabilitation, along with being lonely, as we got older, my mother became mean. I used to watch her go from 0-60 in .05 seconds; and to a 5 year old, that's scary. She would beat my sister so bad, and she was practically handicap. The whippings would be over silly stuff, but my sister never helped the situation because she always talked back. One day, my mom ask her about folding the towels and Rashieta replied too sassy, so, my mom beat her up and down the hallway naked while my sister was on crutches. All I could do was cry and beg my mom to stop. We were in my sister's grandma Elouise's house, so she intervened and stopped my mother from hitting my sister that day.

Life was kind of a blur at this point. I was 5 years old, and saw everything that was happening, but it didn't have meaning to me at this point. My sister, Rashieta, who was now 11 was uptown with her grandmother, Elouise, recovering from multiple surgeries and hospital stays. Her childhood was regaining some normalcy while mine dwindled away. My nana, who I lived with, was retired from Chase after working there 25 years. Her life, day in and day out, was JP Morgan & Chase. After retiring, everything involved beer. Unfortunately, without much priority in her life, her number one priority was drinking when she woke up. She cooked every now and then, but you could expect for the food to be spiked with her 40oz beer of choice. I loved my nana dearly; and although she battled her habits, I was still her 5 year old granddaughter who could do no wrong and was the best hair stylist in town. Every so often, I would catch her watching tv and sneak a style in. Nana would let me part her hair, put grease on her scalp, and put as many ponytails with barrettes as I wanted. I lived for these moments, because when she was up, it was like she was my protection. When my mother was gone, she was the only one to feed me, bathe me, or just even notice me. When she wasn't awake, it was because she was passed out drunk and nothing could wake her up.

I became more familiar with the rest of my family as my nana's drunk spells grew longer. My nana had a 3-bedroom apartment in Frederick Douglass projects, and out of her 5 children, all of them lived with her, except my mom and my aunt,

Gina. My aunt Gina moved away when I was a baby, and never looked back upon New York. My mother had an apartment in the Bronx, and that's where we went when she wanted us all together. My mom would pick me up, and then, we would ride the M100 to get my sister, and we'd ride the BX15 to go to her house in the Bronx. That's where my mom cooked, and where all of our toys were. The building we lived in was up the hill, so it was a long walk from the bus stop. It was an old building, too, and we lived on the first floor apartment that faced the back of a school. My mother never let us go outside because she said it was too ghetto. She even caught someone trying to come in our window once, so she always kept the windows locked. Despite my mother's reservations about the building she lived in, I loved it up there. I loved that me and my sister could play and be kids together when we were HOME.

Back in Harlem, my nana had her own room and her oldest daughter, Martina, had her own room. Martina had a son named, Saeed, and she worked for MTA. Her and her son's father were separated, so they shared custody. Her son would come for a few days out the week, but never for too long. My aunt would lock herself in the room and not come out until she was ready to leave. She never cleaned, cooked, or interacted with us much; and when she wanted to eat she only brought food for herself to eat in her room. I remember, so vividly, being hungry. My nana's room was never locked, but she was the next best thing to dead when she was in one of her drunk comas. My aunt's room was always locked, but we could hear her up watching tv through the door. She rarely responded to my hungry cries; and if her son was there, she would just tell us to wait until it was time for her to go out, and only take him. Eventually, she would get up and leave to go feed him and take him to his dad. I remember being hungry and eating jelly right out the jar with a spoon. That was the only thing in the refrigerator that I could recognize and eat. There were never two foods that matched. Jelly, no peanut butter. Cereal, no milk.

The last room in the house belonged to my Uncle Junior. He was usually high and didn't say much. I was far too young to know what high was or even what drugs were for that matter, I just knew he closed the door, and came out like Superman ready to take on the day. He was always in his room blasting his music, and he only came out to leave. I don't recall him interacting with anyone hardly ever, especially us kids. He would walk out his room and out the front door without even speaking. I honestly don't know much about my Uncle Junior because he was very isolated. I felt like he knew what was going on in the house but just chose to seclude himself and ignore it... which brings me to my last uncle, Troy.

Troy was the baby out of all my nana's children. Troy slept on the couch and came and went as he pleased. He was a troublemaker outside in the streets, but at heart, my nana thought he was out of harm's way if he was around the house. I always felt like I interacted with him the most, because when he was around, he was always nice to me. I grew to learn he was only looking for the opportune time to fuck with me. Troy knew when everyone went to work, when everyone was sleep, when everyone was high, and when everyone was drunk. He was a predator long before anyone knew, and he preyed on me. Troy had a couple of misdemeanors under his belt, but nothing close to what he was truly capable of. He was tall and handsome, which made him a ladies man. You would think with all the attention he got outside the house, he wouldn't want to mess with little ole me. Well, of course, now I know it was nothing but the devil, so the real question was, "why not fuck with me?"

Troy started slow, and he was sneaky. I was young, and he made me trust him. He always had a game for us to play or something cool to watch on TV. When he got comfortable with his surroundings, he would change the game to somehow be about me and him. He knew I liked to do hair and play doctor and shit, so he would act like it was something wrong with him. He would get the Vaseline and say I should rub it on his legs because he was injured. Then, he would pull his penis out and tell me not to be scared, and to put some Vaseline on there, too. I would always get weird when the game turned to shit I didn't understand. I knew it was his private parts because my mom talked to me about my private parts, but I didn't understand why he was always pulling his out. Even if I was just watching TV, he would come sit next to me and take his penis out. One day, his Vaseline dreams escalated, and he was setting up for him to violate me even more. We were in my nana's room watching TV; she wasn't there that day. Aunt Martina was in her room, and so was Junior, but I think Troy knew they weren't coming out to check on me at all. He had on sweatpants and no underwear, and insisted he wanted to show me something, but I couldn't tell anyone...it was our little secret. He made me stand up, and he took my panties off and put them in his pocket. He was already Vaselined up under his sweatpants and he started examining me. He made me lean over the bed and began rubbing his penis on me, and then tried to stick it in. I screamed at the top of my lungs and began crying profusely. He grabbed my mouth and said, "You have to be quiet."

I was only 5, but the memory is like yesterday's thought; because I think this is when I first realized that nobody gave a fuck. I kept being loud, and yelling until it made him uncomfortable and he stopped. No one ever came to check on me to see why I was screaming or crying. My aunt's door never opened, and my Uncle Junior's door was still closed and still blasting music. Troy knew he was in the clear, and every chance he got to fuck with me, he did. He started to make it a habit and I started sticking to my grandmother like glue. Even when she was sleep, I would go in her room and sacrifice not watching what I wanted on TV just to hide out from him. As soon as everyone started leaving or going to sleep I felt like he was looking for me and I was dreading him getting me alone. I prayed for the days my cousin, Saeed, would come over to see his mom. It just meant more people would be in the house and there was no alone time with me. I was scared of Troy; I had to avoid him. After he did it a few more times, he told me I couldn't tell anyone or he would kill me. He even explained how easy it would be to kill me. This went on for some time; and everytime I tried to work up the nerve to tell my mom, he would walk in the room or the bathroom, or creep around from the other side of the wall to give me a mean look as if he knew I was about to tell. I would beg for my mom to take me with her, but she usually was just stopping by to check on me and was right back out the door. One day I was so close to telling her everything, because she asked if anyone had "been down in my privates." (I think my she had a gut feeling, too) I started to say yes, but, then, I saw him creeping around the kitchen wall as we were in the living room; so, I quickly said no. My mom pressed me about it a little more because I think it looked like something was wrong after she gave me a bath, but I kept denying it and changing the subject. She eventually left it alone and went on about her business. I kept avoiding Troy with every ounce of me, because, now, I thought he would kill me just because he knew I was scared and was close to telling on him. I just needed to get my momma alone and I was going to tell everything. I just wanted out as soon as possible. As I got older, I began visiting my sister's grandmother's house more often. It it was so normal over there. But, Troy kept getting too close, and I was out of dodging options.

I had a weekend away with my sister at her grandma's house and I had just gotten back to my nana's house. I was sick, but my mom left quick because she had to go. I had already been sick for a few days, but my mom thought I just needed to lay down and it would pass. I had to take a bath, and my nana asked Troy to run the bath water. I immediately started crying. I was crying because she asked him, and I was crying because I was in pain. I didn't understand then, but I now know it was all God's design. I started throwing up all over the bathroom until it was just blood coming up. I was in so much pain; and I eventually passed out in the bathroom and my nana called the ambulance to come and get me. Just like that, everything ended; and I woke up in the back of an ambulance, scared as hell, looking at my nana, but relieved all in the same thought, because I got away with no bath and no Troy.

Hey, Kid

Manhattan , 1997

I arrived at the nicest Jewish children's hospital that Harlem,
New York had to offer. I didn't fully understand what was
happening, but I knew it was serious because they admitted
me into my own room rather quickly. I was so excited! I was
the epitome of the child who gets to the doctor and isn't sick
anymore. They had all kinds of kid stuff to do and people
walking around entertaining us all day with balloons and magic
tricks. They had great food, and all I had to do was roll my
little IV cart with me and I could go play with the other sick
kids. I was in the hospital a week and did not want to leave. I
had a urinary tract infection that got so bad, it started to affect
my bladder and kidneys. They kept me and nursed me back to
health the whole week on antibiotics, but of course the inevitable
question, "How does a 6 year old get a UTI so bad?" They began
asking my mom questions and even called in child services to
interview me. They took me to the little art room and the social
worker had me draw pictures about my home. My mom insisted
to the doctors and staff that I had just been wiping the wrong
way, and she would emphasize on the proper way to wipe going
forward. My sister's grandmother came to visit and I heard them
already making plans for me to go over to her house. My mother
felt like that was best because my sister was so sickly, and she
did so well with her. My sister's grandmother insisted that my
mom bring me and make the change in my schools. Truth be
told, I think everyone had their own funky suspicions about
someone fucking with me. I was still scared in the hospital, and
all I could think about was Troy killing me. I didn't say anything,
I just wanted to go where my sister was so I could forget it ever
happened and he ever existed.

When we were alone, my mother pressed me about my privates a few more times, but at this point I had made up my mind that I was going to forget it ever happened. My mother never insisted or carried on for a long time anyway, so I knew she would stop asking. I was released from the hospital, and we went back to my nana's house, but I was counting the days until I got to go to my sister's grandmother's house. I kept begging Rashieta to come and get me because I knew she could ride the bus by herself. My nana really didn't care if I went. She was still drinking and barely coherent; and Rashieta's grandmother, Eloise, was ready for me to come. My Uncle Troy had gotten himself into trouble, without any of my help, and was arrested for rape . That was the first of many accusations against him, and he would spend the rest of his days in prison. No one ever knew that I understood so well, but I was happier than ever to overhear that he was in jail. I knew he couldn't kill me in jail, so I felt like I could talk. But, as soon as my sister came to get me, I didn't even care as much anymore. My mother kept stalling; and one day, Rashieta got permission from her grandmother to come uptown to get me for the weekend; but she also had to bring me back. That never happened and I never looked back.

Imagine yourself in Hell...yelling, screaming, and scratching at the walls, and in walks an angel. She grabs your hand and you both walk to the bus stop. In my mind, that's exactly how it happened. One day I was in Hell, and the next day, I wasn't. The bus pulled up in front of MET supermarket, and across the street was building 1305. You would have thought I pulled up to Rodeo Drive. It wasn't a pretty sight. Grant Projects at its finest, but I instantly felt safe. I didn't know what to call it yet, but I felt God all around. I instantly became a kid again. There were children in front of the building playing in the sprinklers, playing double dutch, and my sister had friends. People were yelling her name across the park and walking up to her. Her friends' little sisters wanted to play with me, and, hell, I got to go outside and play. It was amazing, no matter how dirty or disoriented it seemed. I was happy, and I was able to make up for years of not being just a kid.

Our building was 21 floors high, and I felt like my sister knew somebody on every floor. We woke up in the summers and was outside by 10:30am. We never had much food, but that was cool. I never cared, because it was more than what I had at my nana's house and my sister's grandma cooked more often. I was always grateful, even if we ate neckbones consecutively throughout the week. Rashieta hated it, and often got cursed out for complaining; but I didn't dare complain. Especially because I knew if we got lucky on Sunday, her grandmother would bake a yellow cake. I usually had Rashieta's back, but when it came to that, I usually let her get in trouble alone. We had to eat the school free lunch in the summer so we couldn't be late. Some days the food was good and some days it wasn't, but we were lit everyday! On the days we didn't eat the lunch we took the food outside to play house and act like we were cooking .We occasionally played "Jerry Springer" and "Maury," and would throw the food into the fake booing audience. Life was simple, yet, so grand to me. We played outside everyday until the street lights came on and my grandma made Rashieta take me everywhere. I was in a whole new world, and as long as I wasn't in Hell, I was happy.

Tough Love > No Love

Elouise Tribue was the real MVP. We grew up knowing her as my sister's grandmother; however, in all actuality, she didn't have any grandchildren. My sister found out in her 20s, that the man she knew as her dad all her life wasn't her dad after all. But, needless to say, Elouise took us in as her own children and did the best she could with what she had. Elouise was old, but full of spunk. She went outside everyday and sat on the bench in front of the building and gossiped with her friend, Mary. She wore her hair in a ponytail to the side like she was fresh out of junior high, but her hair was 100% gray. She had the spirit of a young bull, and did her best to raise us as young bulls. She knew I was absolutely no kin to her, but she loved me and she made sure I was solid.

6E. Our apartment door was right in front of the elevator (that barely worked and always stank) and the synarator, which always made it extra cold or extra hot. My sister and her grandmother argued about her bringing me there at first, because my mom really didn't officially move me yet. My sister had just come to get me for the weekend, and I never went back. They argued about her taking me back and waiting on my mom, but deep down, though never ever spoken, my grandmother knew I was being abused. She knew something wasn't right, but hell, only a blind person couldn't. Mind you, my grandfather was blind, and my mom used to take us to his house sometimes, but it's hard for a blind man to watch a 5 and 11 year old. My grandfather would talk shit to my mom about leaving us, but it rolled off her shoulders like butter, especially since his verbal lashings were usually accompanied by money. But, neither here nor there, I was a mute child and I was scared to talk.

I was very clingy to my grandmother Eloise, and I think she just knew what I needed at that time. I slept in her bedroom and her wig heads would scare me sitting on the dresser most nights. I would wake her up, to tell her I couldn't sleep, and she would always tell me to "pretend, close your eyes and think about what you want to dream about." She smoked cigarettes and she had asthma. All she watched on TV was The Price is Right, Wheel of Fortune, Tom & Jerry, and News 1. An occasional baseball game was sprinkled throughout, but her main thing was reading her numbers and studying her next play for the next day. She had 2 cats, and 1 slept in the bed with her. Those were her babies, however, she had 2 kids as well.

Eloise had 2 sons, one of which died in his sleep on my birthday (that was who we knew to be my sister's father), and my uncle, Butch. Uncle Butch was the first older man I could be around that I wasn't afraid of. He was the first man to really just love me like a baby girl. My grandma didn't hug or give many "I love you's," but she loved you. It was all tough love. She didn't raise no punks, and she made sure we knew what hard work was.

Grandma Eloise ran away from Tampa when she was 17 to move to New York, and never looked back. She always said she did her own thing, but she was persistent and a hard worker. The job she got when she moved to New York when she was 17 was the job she retired from. It was a leather belt factory, so you know she had a special kind of belts to whip our asses with. Literally, it was a tightly leather coiled cylindrical long rope, that could wrap around you under the bed, and around the corner, if you was trying to run. She emphasized being the best in school, because you could do anything you want in life. She also applied education to everything; down to if you want to go outside or go to sleep, you better do your school work and do it NEAT. Education was first! I felt my grandma was extra hard on me because she knew my sister was a rebel and was going to do her own thing anyway. I tried to hide that my teacher recommended I go to this prestigious academy for 5th grade, and of course I got a whipping. I had been throwing the paper away every time the teacher asked me to bring it home. She went off on me; and yes, I ended up going to Fredrick Douglas Academy the following year.

Needless to say, Elouise talked her shit to my mom about coming to get both her kids, but the conversation about me going back uptown faded away. I don't think I showed it much back then, but I was boiling over with joy. It was still the projects and it still wasn't much food, but it was more than I had before. My grandma would put together meals, but everything was made with love. She didn't have much money so everything was store brand and tasted weird. We ate full meals when we could, and it was usually neck bones and rice(my sister tried to tell her one day we hated neck bones and she cursed her out, & she didn't cook or buy food for like a week. We ate bread & noodles. When we ran out of everything, we started pulling the can goods out trying to make weird food combinations out of what we had. We survived off of free lunch in the summer, so not going was not an option. You went or you didn't eat lunch that day; and dinner was scarce. None of that mattered though. You would have thought I was in Bel-Air the way I felt. It was pure bliss for me. My grandmother taught me "Don't nobody in this world gotta do nothing for you, down to you getting icey money from me. I do it because I want to but, don't ever expect it and remain grateful." I learned my most valuable morals through her tough love. I had my first birthday party when I was 8 years old, with cake and ice cream (that was the best feeling ever!!). I met my best friend, Imani, in 2nd grade (that's still my girl). I followed my sister everywhere and wanted to be just like her, (but I was kind of a punk) and she was a young firecracker, so that was hard! Some would have called my sister a rebel, but to me, she was a go getter. She always made it happen, and no matter what she wanted in life, she went after it. She eventually taught me how to fight, because she fought a lot. Her enemies had little sisters who wanted to fight me, and I couldn't fight. I was scared, but that changed, too. My grandma was a fighter, too. I remember her telling me, "Ain't no punks in this house; and if your sister fights, then you fight!" That is a scary statement to a kid who is already insecure and very timid. My sister used to whip me for everything, from eating candy, down to not writing with my right hand, even though I was really left handed. She didn't know any better; she was mean and beat me, I believe, because that's all my mom did to her.

My Uncle Butch had his own type of tough love, too. He was the only positive male figure I had in my life, so I loved when he came to visit us. He would tickle me and always have pocket change for us to have. My uncle was stern, though, and didn't take no shit. I remember the time he choked Rashieta out because she came in the house at 6 A.M., rolled her eyes, and said, "So?" He snapped on her, and reminded her that she wasn't grown. I remember that fight, because my sister moved out not too long after that. My grandma's house was about principle and respect. The only thing I ever got a whipping for (outside of when my sister got me in trouble) was breaking the lamp and lying about it. My grandma made sure to tell me after I was blistered up, "Don't you ever lie to me. I beat you because you lied." I went on to love my grandmother more than anything in the whole world. Everything was tough love, but I took it all in; and when I could steal a hug and be mushy, I would. She would still tell me to get off of her, but it still felt good. My mom had made it a habit of calling to say she was coming to get us and never showing up. My grandma used to be pissed, because she knew we were living with her full-time, and she didn't sign up for that; but this went on for years, so I learned to take the only love I could get. I learned alot from my grandma, and although she didn't have much to give, she had a lot of love. Her mannerisms spoke love, and she moved effortlessly. No matter how she felt about having two kids just dropped off on her, she always made sure we were good. We were her kids, too.

Adult Starts Now

Harlem 2002

This was the first time in my life I could admit I was feeling myself. I had my own friends, and I was finding my own way. I had gotten my first boyfriend that I met at church. That didn't last long though. He tried to tongue kiss me; and I got so grossed out, because it was way too much spit. I dumped him right after that experience. He couldn't call my house and speak to me anyway, because my grandma wasn't having it; so we barely spoke. But yes, more importantly, I was feeling myself. My sister was now 17, and had moved out to Atlanta, Georgia. I had my own room now. I was going to Frederick Douglass Academy, so I had independence with riding the train and the bus by myself. Me and my friend, Imani, could skip school if we wanted to, or be extra late just because we wanted breakfast. I had gotten into a couple fights, so I was more confident in myself now, too. I didn't need my sister to back me up, even though I was still a little punk on the inside. I was coming into myself, and I just wanted to be a teenager; although I was only 12. I already had gotten my period, and that made me feel even more like a teenager. So, theoretically, you couldn't tell me shit.

Rashieta was living in Atlanta, and I can't even lie, I missed her a lot. She wrote me and my grandma letters talking about how things were and how my mom was treating her. My mom had already been living in Atlanta with her boyfriend; and Rashieta moved down there with her friend as a roommate. It was weird not having her in the house or on the block, but I know she wanted to try living on her own. My grandma would send encouraging letters that was full of tough love and spunk like, "Don't let shit get you down," or "Keep going, and you are going to be just fine." Even though my sister was gone, I still had her friends who were like my sisters, because we were so close.

Shaquana was Rashieta's best friend, and she always made sure I was that good.

At this time, I was in the sixth grade; and it was starting to get hot outside, so I wanted to look cute. I didn't have many clothes, and I didn't have many sneakers. All I had was what my sister brought me before she left for Atlanta. It was the last day of school, and on my way home, I wanted to stop by Shaquana's house so that I could borrow her jean dress and some other clothes from her twin sister. No one was home, so I cut through the neighborhood on the way to our apartment. Uncle Butch had just told me not to cross through this neighbor because of the abandoned buildings. Someone could easily snatch me up, he said. But, I was being lazy; and I didn't feel like walking the long way. That day, my hard head made a soft ass. I got hit by a car. The car was passing through the light that had just turned red from green, and I heard a man call out, "Little girl, watch out!" As I heard the stranger yell at me, I stepped back and turned around at the same time, and the truck rolled over my right leg. I instantly fell to the ground and cried out for help. I think I was more mad that I was caught where I wasn't supposed be more than I was mad about being hit. I knew I would have to explain why I was on that street by myself. Another stranger called the ambulance, and they had to come to take me to the Harlem Hospital. I was scared to give my grandma's phone number because I was wrong, and, because my leg was broke. I knew it was serious because I couldn't walk, and it looked crazy. Both my tibia and fibula were broken and sticking out through my skin. In the ambulance, all I could think about was how much trouble I was going to be in. When I got to Harlem Hospital, I was surprised that my grandma showed up with a smile, as opposed to a frown. She asked where I was going and what I was doing, but I just said that I was walking home from school with a friend. I never mentioned that I was going to Shaquana's house, because I hadn't asked to go to her house . My sister had gotten word that I got hit by a car, but of course, when word goes through random people, they get the worst side of a very fabricated story.

They told my sister that the car ran over my head and that I was on life support. She rushed to New York in a panic, because she thought that my injuries were way more serious than they were. Rashieta got there a lot quicker than my mom did; and she brought my favorite—a McDonald's Mcflurry with a double cheeseburger and fries. I was so happy to see her. All of this happened the week before July 4th, so Rashieta decided to stay in New York for the holiday.

I was in the hospital for a week after surgery on my leg. By the time they let me go home, my mom had made it to New York; and it was weird, because I always felt like my mom found a way to put herself before me. For example, she came and saw that I was in a cast all the way up to my thigh and I had to have my foot elevated in the bed, and she still made me sleep on the couch, because she wanted to sleep in my bed for her back. I was 12 years old, so of course, I didn't saying anything; but it bothered me. She and my sister still had their funky attitude towards each other; and it just blew off the whole energy of everything. On July 4th, my grandma needed a refill of her asthma pump, and I was usually the one who went and got it. However, since I had broke my leg, I couldn't go to her pharmacy anymore. My grandma sent Rashieta; and when she came back with the medicine, she got ready to go out . That night, as my sister was in the mirror getting ready to step out for the evening, I was in my bed leaning against the window trying to stay cool because it was a real humid night. My grandma had an asthma attack and we had to call 911. Right after we called 911, we called Uncle Butch; but it was a busy night in the city so I felt like it took everyone so long to get there. The EMTs had lots of stuff with them, and it took them forever to get on the elevator and up to our floor with all of it, and back down on the elevators. I watched my grandmother die in the hallway in front of the elevator as they tried to resuscitate her. They were calling for the elevator, but every time it came, it was full. I wanted to scream for people to get off, and they eventually did move some people off after, like, the third elevator came and went. I knew it was

over in that hallway; and I watched as they drove off without the sirens. As I stared out the window, I let a tear fall down my cheek. I couldn't help but think that all the negative energy in the house contributed to her just letting go and going to be with God. I was hurt, and I really didn't know how to express it, because no one really talked to me about anything.

The funeral came quick. I couldn't even get up to look at the body. I didn't want to look doofy with my big ole cast up to my thigh; and I couldn't look at the body because it made me sick. I felt like I died that day, too. It was all a blur to me. I didn't really get to grieve because, now, my mom had to take her child; and that meant, I would moving to Atlanta. I was sad on top of sad. I had to leave my friends along with everything I knew; and on top of that, my grandma was my angel that saved me, and with her gone, I felt like it was right back into Hell for me. I had to grow up, and there was no one to baby me anymore. My grandma didn't baby me alot, but she still allowed me to be a kid. Now, all that kid shit was out the window; and I didn't really have a chance to even cry. I felt like it was my fault, because if I didn't stress my grandma out by getting hit by a car, she wouldn't have had the asthma attack. I was disobedient altogether, and for some weird reason, I felt like God was teaching me a lesson. I know that wasn't the case, but it was just how I felt at the moment. I cried almost daily, and no one knew it. I was mad at myself and the world. I just couldn't understand why God would do this to me. Why would he take her away and move me away to Atlanta to be so unsettled and homeless. It was an out of body experience; and I was numb. I felt like my mom had died; only to find out later, that would be much worse.

Reality = Nightmares
Atlanta 2002

At this point in my life, I would have much rather been dead. It was hard to explain how I felt, but I knew I was sad, and I didn't feel anything. It was like life was happening too fast around me; and I felt like my soul died with my grandma that day. It was a hot summer in July 2002, and I was waving goodbye to all my friends and everything that I had ever known in the city. I had never even been out of the city limits; I barely even went to Jersey. Yet, here I was, two weeks after my grandma's funeral, moving to Atlanta, sad as ever, with no say in anything. It was almost like I was a doll. Something that had no brain, no feelings, and no heart; and I was just being packed up and shipped off. I still had a big cast on my leg, too, so I was extremely uncomfortable, to say the least.

When I got to Atlanta, that's when shit really hit the fan. I didn't really know what my mom did for a living, I just knew that she was inconsistent in calling and coming to see us. I never really knew how bad off she was doing. I was 12 years old, so I really didn't fully understand everything I was seeing, but I was seeing a lot. I remember getting to Atlanta and being with my sister in her car. We went to McDonald's to get a cheeseburger, and they made my cheeseburger with mustard and ketchup. I Immediately spit it out.

"YUCK! What is this and why would they put mustard on my burger?" I yelled.

I quickly learned that I was in the south. From the burger to air—everything was different. Eventually, Rashieta had to drop me back off to my mom's house, because my mom was taking me to physical therapy for my leg. After a few weeks of being at my mom's house, I realize she was being evicted. I saw the first couple of notices on the door, but I didn't read them.

I knew it was real when we came home one day, and everything was outside . My heart dropped. I didn't know what to do or what to think. I was just observing my mom and her actions, and thinking about what we were about to do. She picked up the little stuff that she could (that she felt was important) and she put it in the car. Her friend's car, that is; because we had to call her friend to come pick us up after we got off the bus and saw everything outside. The next few weeks were us staying with different men. Some, I think, were friends; and some, I think, were just men she hadn't talked to in awhile that were doing her a favor. I was able to come and sleep on the couch. She had a best friend, and she was cool, but she stayed with her man in a small one bedroom apartment, so we couldn't sleep there. We only saw her in the day time .

I remember the night, after the second week, that I cracked. I wasn't into spiritual things or praying, but I knew that I needed a savior. I was laying on some man's couch, and he barely addressed me or said hello upon entering his home. Mind you, I was still big, and slow, and handicap, with a cast up to my thigh. His energy immediately displaced mine. My mom gave me a blanket and showed me where I could lay on the couch. She, then, went in the room with him for the night. I was laying there digesting it all. We were homeless, and I still didn't have a chance to really grieve the fact that my grandmother died a month ago! Before I knew it, a tear rolled down my cheek, and my soul was crying. I didn't even know I could be so sad. All I kept wondering was why wouldn't my grandma take me with her; especially if all of this was going on. I got up to find my mom's phone. I had been calling my sister to keep her updated, but only when I could get to a phone. I called, and as always, she was that savior, again. She could tell I had been crying. She asked was I okay and I told her no. She asked me where I was, and I said, "I don't know. We are somewhere different, with someone new." She told me to get up and look for mail and give her the address. My mom didn't know I was leaving until my sister was at the door. When my sister arrived she asked, "What are you doing here?"

Rashieta replied, "I was going to take Shawana with me for tonight."

My mom looked puzzled and thought about it for a second, but she didn't have much words. I guess she felt like she wouldn't address the reason at that moment; and she let me go in peace.

Grow or Die

Depressed, and on my last leg, I felt weak; and my mind was filled with so many bad, tearful thoughts. At this age, I didn't know what depression was, but I knew I didn't feel right. It was now a time in my life that I would have to make a decision to grow or die. I'll be honest, I chose to die first. But, God intervened and showed up full force, even tho I didn't recognize him.

Rashieta had come to get me in her boyfriend's truck. We drove back to his house, and I never looked back. We only met up with my mom when I had to go to the doctor or physical therapy. My mom didn't complain because it was easier for her to move around without me. My sister stayed with her boyfriend full-time and worked at an oil change shop. Her boyfriend worked for the airport. He had a second bedroom with just some sneakers in it, and he let me sleep in there on an air mattress. I cried every night. Yes, I was happy my sister came for me, but I was still unhappy because I missed my grandma. It was like I was the only one who still missed her; and I didn't understand why she left me here in this crazy world. Everything was still going so fast. I had to just blend in and be the kid that wasn't there as I went everywhere with my sister. I was over it. By the time all these feelings bubbled up, I was silently crying, again. I felt like my soul was broken. I didn't want to be here anymore. I had made up my mind that night. I was going to go with my grandma, and there was no looking back. My next decision I had to make was how I was going to kill myself , because I was really still a punk. I had thought about slitting my wrist, but quickly decided against that. I didn't want to feel any pain, and I wanted to go peacefully in a twisted weird sense. I got up and dragged my heavy leg to the bathroom. I grabbed all the pills out of the cabinet, and poured them into a Tylenol bottle. I grabbed a bottle of water and took it back in the room. I had decided I was just going to take all the pills and go to sleep, and I would just wake up with my grandma. No one would miss me, and I would be so happy. As I took the first pill, a lot of cussing and fussing started to arise. I heard a loud thump, and realized my sister and her boyfriend were fighting. By this time, I was scared; but I wanted to get up to see what was happening. Rashieta came rushing in the room during my great debate with fear and said, "Get up!! Let's go!! We are leaving!" She grabbed all my stuff and started heading downstairs to his car. Everything was moving so damn fast I thought to myself, "Damn, I can't even kill myself." God had other plans for me, because he intervened that night; and kept intervening until I lost the thought.

It was weird, because, we left in Rashieta's boyfriend's truck. I guess he felt guilty about getting physical with her, but we left that night and went to her friend's Charice's house. Charice had three little boys all under the age of 8, and a roommate. It was a lot going on there, too. I didn't have time to kill myself so I gave up and sunk into a deeper depression .

Summer was over and it was time for school. My mom enrolled me in school by Rashieta's house in College Park. I was still mad at the world, and I felt very ugly. I was going into the 7th grade; my front two teeth were chipped, I had gotten my cast taken off, but I still had a short leg boot for the first day of school. I quickly became labeled a mean girl from New York. I didn't smile because of my teeth, and I stopped doing my work in school because I was angry. I was a mute, and I didn't do shit. I didn't want to do anything because I missed my grandma, and I missed my friends in New York. I was also sad because when I did talk, the other kids teased me about my teeth. I just wanted to sink into a hole and disappear. It had gotten bad. I just showed up for attendance; and I was the bad ass. Eventually, the teachers called my sister and told on me. I had gotten to the point where I was failing every class. My sister yelled at me . She didn't understand why I was failing since I was a straight "A" student in New York. I was on my "fuck the world, and school, and everything in it" mentality. I was just angry, so I didn't feel like I needed to do work. All my energy was going into being angry, and all my sister's energy was going into me.

Rashieta never took me back to my mother, so she just adjusted her life to having a teenager and having a roommate at 19. My sister started with what she knew best, and she hit me where it hurt...my ego. I was already insecure, so she knew how she had to break me down, and it started with my appearance. I was rude and disrespectful, so I didn't have any good answers the day my sister questioned me about failing every class. She took every piece of clothing I had that night, down to the socks and shoes I had on. She yelled and told me to get out the house just as I was. I had on an undershirt, underwear and socks (she gave me the socks back). I stood outside like that for what felt like hours. I eventually scrunched down real tight in a fetal position next to the door so other people couldn't see me as they were driving through the apartment complex. My sister's roommate came home and they argued about me being outside with no clothes on as a punishment. She didn't always agree with how Rashieta parented, but my sister went with what she knew best. I was invited back in the house, but I wasn't given any of my clothes back. All of my clothes were actually in a trash bag at this point, and I still had to attend school the next day. Rashieta gave me one outfit and a deadline. I couldn't have any of my clothes back until I was passing every class and proved it. I went to school the next day, sad, and more beat down than before. Again, there was a choice to be made—be a bum or get right and, at least, get your clothes back. I went up to my teacher's desk at the end of every class that day and asked how I could bring my grade up. My science teacher, in particular, talked major smack and naturally gave me a hard time. My science teacher along with all my other teachers were intrigued that I was ready to do work now. I stayed after school and began to bust it out. I was far from dumb, just a little disturbed for my age. As you can imagine, I wasn't able to pull up all my grades overnight, and I still only had one outfit. I skipped school the rest of the week. My sister wouldn't even give me a different shirt to wear and I couldn't risk being seen in the exact same clothes as the day before. I rode the school bus to school, and as we exited the bus in the morning, I walked down the side of the school and found a spot to hide until classes started. At the end of the day, I went into school and told the teachers I was sick, but I had my work. They began to take it, and, of course, grade it slowly. By the 3rd day, I was dirty, and kinda starting to stink, too. I begged for, at least, a clean shirt. Rashieta agreed; so I went to regular class on the 4th day, and stayed in for lunch. I did as much make up work as I could possibly do in one sitting. By Friday, I skipped the better half of the day and came in at the end and turned in the rest of my work. My teachers were surprised, because I knew they thought I was slow, but they quickly realized I was just disobedient. I went home that weekend and finished strong, I did every piece of make up work and extra credit, and then some. My grades slowly crept back up into passing and I was rewarded with 2 outfits to where next week. This was probably the only time in my life I would have been thankful for a uniform. My english teacher felt insulted by my disobedience, so upon her taking my work she made it contingent upon me being in the spelling bee. I was livid to say the least. She wanted me to stand in front of people and open my mouth!! What if they saw my teeth!? What if they stared at me!? This was the last task that would get me over the hump to passing, so I agreed, because I knew I wanted my damn clothes back. I went into the spelling bee, then to the finals, all the way into the next semester and WON. I know... crazy, right? God had a sense of humor. I was back to passing every class with flying colors, as one semester ended, and the next began. My teeth were still chipped, and I was still living with my sister's friend and her 3 kids.

As soon as I found myself on the up and up, Rashieta and her roommate started to drift apart. It started with petty differences, and eventually escalated into a full-on fist fight. I watched the whole thing, and I knew we were moving that night.

They argued; and Rashieta tried to stay cool as her friend became irate. Her friend started to push and curse her out. I think she hit my sister one too many times, because she snapped. Rashieta knocked her front teeth clean out her mouth on the second punch. By this point, me and all the kids were screaming, just watching the blood come from her mouth. Her roommate's boyfriend was there and he came late to break it up. By this time, her roommate noticed her teeth upon the floor and she started yelling for us to get out. The school year was just about over; and so was our stay with her roommate.

Mother vs Sister
Atlanta, 2013

Love...hate...then, hate again. My mother's and sister's relationship towards each other was never good, and I can't even lie, it made me a little bias growing up. My sister was born handicap, and had multiple surgeries before the age of 6. Her father died the exact same day I was born. My mom went into the mental hospital for a few months. She eventually found herself again, and was able to come and get her kids (I was in Belize, and Rashieta was at her grandma's house). My mother was never the same, though; and she never really treated my sister right. She would beat Rashieta senseless until she got tired; but, mind you, my sister had consistent leg surgeries throughout her whole life. Most of the time, Rashieta was on crutches; and when she wasn't on crutches, she was walking with a limp. My mom still always asked her to do everything, especially when it pertained to me. It was like my mother was blind to the fact that my sister couldn't do normal tasks at a normal pace, and she would snap. I remember plenty of times when my grandmother had to intervene because she was beating her so bad. But, Rasheita was strong, and she always shook it off. Time passed and our mom grew more distant as she moved away to Atlanta, and left us in New York with our grandma. My mother would call and still try to regulate and discipline through the phone from miles away. Before you knew it, 3 years had passed and we hadn't seen her. She was like that dad who would call and say he was on the way, but never showed up. As you can imagine, when she did decide to show her face, my sister didn't have much respect for her; and on top of that, my sister was just rude. Myself on the other hand, I loved my mom dearly; and even after 3 years of not seeing her, I was still so happy when she came. My dislike for her grew with her actions towards my sister, and just us as children, in general.

When Rashieta moved away to Atlanta, she would write and tell my grandma about her experiences with my mom, and it made me sad. I hated the way my mom treated my sister, and as I grew older, I didn't like my mom much, because I felt like she was selfish and never put us first.

Fast forward to 8th grade year. I was living with my sister full-time. I was going to school while my sister worked on cars at Jiffy Lube. We had our apartment, and it was just us. My sister was busting her ass and was always at work. I was still an angry kid, but a little less depressed. I wasn't trying to kill myself anymore, but I still had my insecurities about myself. I hated my face during this time in my life, because puberty got the best of me. Rashieta tried hard to make sure I was fly and comfortable. Whatever she didn't make at work, was supplemented by the men she dated that would give her money, take us out to eat, and buy me whatever I asked for. It was to the point that if I needed something, Rashieta would tell me to ask her during dinner when we were out with her male friends. Before we would get home from the date, I would have whatever I was asking for at dinner. It was strategic and brilliant, to say the least. I didn't want for much, and we were surviving. I went to school and got good grades, and that was all she ever really asked for. I was young and naive, so my middle school friends weren't the ideal friends for me. I started to get ahead of myself with the wrong influences and all the extra unmonitored time. My friends were ghetto and grown, but I had one friend that stayed a few doors down from me, and she introduced me to all the "fast" shit. She had more than one boyfriend, and grown men, too. She dressed very sexy and was crazy as hell. I remember one night, in particular, that I almost died following this girl. She asked me to walk with her to the next neighborhood and I thought nothing of it because this was my friend. We got over there, and I realize she was scooping to see if this grown ass man she was talking to had another girl over. And, he DID!!!! So, she got mad and poured her koolaid in his gas tank. I was completely shocked. He came outside as she was trying to bust his tires, and I ran off. I started leaving her and she soon followed cursing me out. I was scared because I knew she was wrong as hell. I knew he sold drugs and would shoot at her, most likely. As soon as we got to her house, she called him, again, and they started arguing; and he sure did tell her he was going to kill her ass and he would be over to her house. I didn't tell her that night as I left quickly to go home, but I was over our friendship. I started hitting some other friends up and started feeling myself.

Although I had my own mind, and my sister didn't buy, nor allow me to wear anything revealing, the bad traits still rubbed off on me. I started to feel more secure in myself, but not beautiful as I should feel. I wanted to feel sexy and appealing to the opposite sex. I lost my virginity to that same crazy ass friend's older brother; and still regret it. It hurt so bad, and he dumped me, like, a week after. Talk about a way to fuck up a person's emotions just when I thought I was back on track. I didn't have sex again for, like, a year. I had really bad periods after I started having sex, and it was like I got my period twice a month. I passed out in the bathroom from losing so much blood one day, and ended up having to go to the hospital. That's when Rashieta found out I had had sex. I was a mess, and I had to tell her. She didn't say much, but she killed my whole summer, and sent me to New York because she couldn't watch me and go to work. When I returned from New York, I was at Rashieta's house a few weeks; but, her and my mom had been going back and forth since the hospital thing. Rashieta was also angry because she just wanted my mom to help us out a little more. My mom got food stamps for me, but wouldn't buy food for me. She wouldn't let my sister borrow her card or even buy us a gallon of milk. Eventually, this disagreement kept recurring and escalated. One day, my mom came over to the house with her friend, Kelly, and they argued. It started about the milk and food that she wouldn't buy us, but it quickly escalated to a respect issue for my mom. My sister felt like she didn't need to respect my mom. They exchanged words and my mom tried to hit my sister, and they starting fighting. Like, fist fighting. My jaw hit the floor. I was shocked; and my mom's friend didn't intervene at all. I guess, because she felt my sister was wrong. My mom left with her friend and went to the police station and pressed charges on Rashieta. She was pretty bruised up and they took pictures. They came back with the police and arrested my sister. I was devastated. Everything happened so quick. I was pissed that my mom had gotten the police involved, and was allowing them to put Rashieta, my savior, in jail! My dislike grew even more for my mom, and I didn't want to go live with her. The police left with Rashieta, and I was crying. My mom came back in the house and told me to pack up and started talking shit about how I needed to live with her anyway because I look ghetto (she was referring to my bunny rabbit Jordans) and was turning into this ghetto child. All while I'm listening to her, I'm thinking to myself, How long have you not been concerned about where I lived? I grew up in one of the worst projects in Harlem, and have been homeless in the most random places and shelters since living in Atlanta with you. My mom had one bedroom, and the only place I had to sleep, was the couch. I was over her shit talk. I packed my stuff and went out the patio door in the kitchen while the police, my mom, and her friend were all in the living room. I ran away, and I didn't look back.

Now, I will be honest, I didn't think this through at all. It wasn't until I was tired of walking that I started to think about what's next, and who's number did I know by heart. I walked until I got to a store where I could use the phone. I called Rashieta's friend, Charice (YES! The friend that she fought and knocked her teeth out), and broke down. They weren't back to being best friends, but they were on speaking terms. I didn't know who else to call, and I knew she was older than Rashieta, and still cared, so she would help me. I cried and told her Rashieta was in jail, and I had ran away. I also asked if I could come to her house. She immediately came and got me. I explained everything that happened; and I thought right, because my sister eventually used her one phone call to call Charice. She told Rashieta I was there with her, but also explained my mother would come looking for me and was probably going to send the police. I spent the night at Charice's house; but when I woke up the next morning, she sat me down to talk. She explained the magnitude of what was happening and that, yes, she was going to help Rashieta get out of jail, but I wouldn't be able to go back to her house. I had to make a choice. Either, I was going back to my mom's house, or turn myself in and look into emancipation. I wouldn't be able to go to my sister at all. I was angry with my mom so I took the hard, high road. She dropped me off down the street, and I walked myself into DFCS directly. I told them my mom was neglecting me while I had been living with my sister, and my mom had her arrested. In my mind, I thought they would hear my story and cries and let me start the process of being emancipated. I was wrong and uninformed. They shut my little perfect dreams and plans down. DFCS sent me straight to a group home and opened up an investigation on my mom.

I was in an all girls group home for what felt like forever. But, in reality, it was only 2 months. The group home felt like jail, and I was right back to being depressed. I had a new way of channeling my depression, though. I just took it out on the people around me. I was mean, and anybody could get it by this point. I had all my cute Pepe jeans and sneakers with me, so I had to fight to protect myself and my stuff. That, in itself, turned me into a monster. I felt like I was already dealing with my own emotions, and then somebody had the audacity to try to steal what little, fly, clothes I had. I snapped; and I was in there taking bitches' head off, because I didn't want them to think they could keep trying me. Honestly, it was a good release. I stood my ground and made sure everybody knew what was up-from the other foster girls, down to the staff who watched us. I hated when they made us sit in a room together. I didn't want to do any group therapy shit or anything remotely close. So, eventually, they just let me be separated because I was bucking everything in sight, and I was liable to swing on someone. My antics got me released with a first class ticket to mandatory therapy and counseling, because by the time they released me, they thought

I was bat shit crazy. I was going crazy in my own thoughts. They released me to my mom, who took me straight to Rashieta because she had shit to do (ironically); but she definitely lectured the whole way about how I couldn't live with Rashieta anymore. She said that I had brought all this drama into her life because they were investigating her; and she already had plans to enroll me in school in Gwinnett County. I was pissed and still wasn't with the shit. By this time, I had my own, full grown, hate for my mom; and she felt like it was all my sister's influence, but she had her fair share to do with it, as well. I stayed with Rashieta for the weekend, and she explained why I needed to simmer down, because I had definitely made the block hot and she already had a case, and now the people were all in our business. My mother had the same conversation, again, with me driving home...about the people being all in her business, and how she really didn't like that shit because she was a legend in the scamming world. That's how we survived...licks and public assistance. I talked back and did not express much concern about fucking up the money. I remember, so vividly, my mother cursing me out and pushing my head into the car window as she threatened to pull over and drag me out the car and kill me. It was definitely one of those, "I brought you in this world and I can take you out" moments. I was full of angry tears, and cried the whole way home. My mom still had a small, one bedroom apartment, so I slept on the couch. It's crazy how I never felt at home staying with my her. I hated my new school and everything around me. I was mean, and didn't talk to much of anyone. I soon became the mean girl from New York, here, as well. Me and my mom argued everyday, because she was OCD and had a problem with everything I did, down to how I breathed. I was sick of her shit all over again. I packed up my stuff and almost ran away again. It was after another argument, and I was going to pour out all the rubbing alcohol and set the apartment on fire before I walked out. I called my sister crying, and told her what I was about to do. She told me to leave all my shit and walk out now. She knew I had snapped... again. And, I was REALLY about to set probably the whole damn apartment building on fire, with my momma in it. She told me to walk across the street and she would drive to get me. I didn't find out until she got there, but she had a guy friend that stayed in the same apartments as my mom, so he invited us into his home that evening for dinner. After dinner, she walked me home because I still had school the next day, but she promised to come get me for the weekend. My mom even tried to stop my weekend getaways, but my sister and mother finally found some common ground (I think she really told my mom I was losing it at one point), which further made my mom push the mandatory therapy sessions. All of the DFCS home visits had stopped, but they wouldn't close the case until I went to the mandatory therapy, because I showed my ass so much in the group home, and on paper, I was just deemed a disturbed little child. The state paid up a couple months of therapy and wouldn't release the case until the doctor signed off on it.

In my mind, I was telling myself, I don't need no damn shrink! Only crazy people need shrinks, and I'm not crazy. My mother and sister agreed, for once in their life, that I needed to talk to someone. I was pissed, because now I thought they were ganging up on me, and going to the shrink would make me crazy. I was so angry, (like most of the time) but, needless to say, my mother found a small psychiatrist medical office in Gwinnett next to the hockey arena and Thursdays were my day.

It's Okay to Cry

North Gwinnett, 2004

Dr. Floyd was a very pretty and poised black woman. She was smart and very professional. That was my first impression of her, so off the rip, she couldn't relate to shit that I had been through or tell me anything about how I was "feeling".

"How are you, Shawana? Tell me about yourself," Dr. Floyd asked at the beginning of each session. I completely shut down every Thursday. She would ask question after question, and I gave her nothing. I would just sit there and stare. I was tough as steel for the first month. I did not talk, or answer any questions. Dr. Floyd tried to talk to me with my mother in and out of the sessions. After 30 minutes of me refusing to talk, she would call my mother in and I would just listen to my mother answer her questions. It usually didn't do anything but make me more mad, because my mom and her would just be talking about shit they knew nothing about. For example, Dr. Floyd wanted to know why was I so angry, and all my mom could ever mention was my sister, and how my sister was brainwashing me with thoughts to not like her. It was like, in her mind, I had the perfect childhood and she always made sure everything was good; and that just wasn't how I saw it. Hell, fuck it, that just wasn't how it was. I held on to my silence a good 5 weeks, but Dr. Floyd wore me down to the bone. She invited my sister to sessions because she thought it would help, but my sister never showed up. That was asking for too much, and Dr. Floyd knew it, so she stopped asking.

The day I broke, it started in a session with my mom. She was reliving this perfect childhood in one of her stories, and I didn't even know it ,but I had started cry. My soul was crying, and I didn't even notice until they stopped talking to offer me tissue. I took the tissue and checked my emotions. I immediately suited back up in defense and the questions were fired at me, again. I didn't speak that session, because we ran out of time, but Dr. Floyd knew she had reached new ground. I felt like the next Thursday came quicker than it ever did before, and as soon as we walked in, she asked my mother to excuse herself, and she was on my neck. I had to give her credit, we were 6 weeks in and she was one of the most persistent and resilient individuals I had ever met, because I wasn't polite. She started with, "Shawana, I just want to get to know you and what could make a beautiful girl like you cry."

I felt like she was trying to be a little funny because I was always so tough all of the time. At this point, I was embarrassed because I cried; she found my weakness, and she knew it. I was a freshman in high school, and that was the way I found peace, by not feeling emotion. I never exchanged I love you's, or kisses and hugs often with my sister or my mother. Never, actually. So, I was always on tough girl mode. I didn't show any feelings, because I felt people really don't care about your feelings, they just want you to go with the flow and don't fuck up the routine; and I learned that young. Dr. Floyd tapped back into to my emotions, and she was brilliant at it. She started with the obvious, but then went on to tell me about myself and her impressions of me and who I was. I grew very defensive and...boom! She had me.

"You don't know me, so don't act like you do," I said.

Of course, she went into, "I want to know you. I want to know what makes you upset with your mom?"

It started there. I wanted her to really know I didn't hate my mom because of my sister, that shit was way deeper than rap with me. I was just over the sessions, and ready to chuck the deuces. I felt like if I said what was on my mind, she would take it as enough, and let us be done. So, on that Thursday, we went over time because she let me have the whole hour. The only thing I asked was that we be in private, because I wanted to give her the real, and these were things I honestly never spoke out loud. Everything I was about to say had never made it a second out of my thoughts. Honestly, I was so emotionally drained, I couldn't help but cry. I was trying so hard to stop crying, but I couldn't stop. It was like my secrets, hate, emotions, and memories were boiling over on the inside, and that's where the water for my tears were coming from. I shrugged my shoulders. "What you want to know?" I asked, as I wiped away tears. She asked me to tell her what makes me cry, and I replied, "Everything."

Dr. Floyd then asked "What did your mom do?"

I replied, "Not enough."

"What does that mean?" she probed.

I started at the beginning; my perspective on my mom being busy and always gone. I told her about how my sister and I were separated, at first, living with our grandmothers, while our mom had an apartment in the Bronx. Dr. Floyd asked all the probing questions; and all the answers were sad and unfortunate. I explained how my uncle used to touch me and have dry sex with me. I told her about me being hospitalized, and me feeling like my grandmother and everyone knew. I went on to tell her how my mom was always mean to my sister and that's why they argue. My grandmother died and I was forced out of New York down to Atlanta. We were evicted, homeless, and moved around alot, all while I had a cast up to my thigh. I told her how my sister came to the rescue, and why I ran away and turned myself into DFCS the way I did. We talked about my anger for my mom stemming from how she treated my sister, because I felt like I loved her, so she needed to love her like she taught us we should love each other. We went back and forth with questions and answers for a whole hour. I told her everything except about my fake suicide attempt, because I, honestly, just tried to forget about that low point of my life. I was older now, and I knew I couldn't go be with my grandma, so I just had to keep rocking because she was watching. I told her I was very depressed when my grandmother died, and it resulted in a deep, long cry. She hugged me. That was the first time I had been hugged in a long time, in a genuine way. I completely broke down and I sobbed like a baby. I hadn't cried like that in a long time, either. She held me tight and told me it was okay to cry. Sometimes, you gotta cry to recharge and start to feel better. She let me cry for what felt like forever, and only God knows how much I truly appreciated her for that.

Dr. FLoyd invited my mom back in so we could close out, but she wanted to share my thoughts with my mom. At this point, the cat was out the bag, so I didn't give a fuck. I told Dr. Floyd she could tell her how I felt. My mother cried, and I could tell her feelings were hurt. She began to express to Dr. Floyd how she always did her best, and she told her to talk directly to me. I understood shit was hard, because I knew what my family did for a living, and I knew what it was like to take losses and to be without. BUT, I let her know all the things I felt like she should have knew, especially, after I was hospitalized for a UTI at 5 years old. Even though he's in jail for life, I still felt like it was just brushed under the rug. Of course, she wanted to know why I didn't tell her, and I let her know that I was just scared. When he told me he would kill me, I believed him, and every time I got ready to say something, he would walk in the room. I never had ample space and opportunity to tell, and then when I finally got out of the house, I just tried to forget. This was actually my first time speaking it out loud since it happened. Our time was definitely way over, but Dr. Floyd wasted no time penciling us in for more therapy sessions.

The ride home was awkward, but it was the best I had felt in a long time. I had felt free and my "fuck it" was at an all time high. I felt like Dr. Floyd cared about me and admired me. Although, this was all in a day's work, I could feel she was genuine. My mom brought up Law and Order, and how there is no statute of limits on crimes like that, but I was honest enough to say that I was just happy he was in jail for life. I had grown to trust Dr. Floyd, and we were honest with each other. I don't think she'll ever know how much she had to do with saving my mind. I wasn't crazy, but I had been holding a lot in and I think she nurtured me out of the improper balance of emotions, guilt, and shame that I carried. I don't know why I was ashamed, but she taught me that I was a tough little girl, and to give myself credit, even when I cry. It was okay to cry; yet, she respected why

I was so tough. She focused less on fixing me and my mom, and more on me just rejuvenating my spirit. We grew, and before I knew it, my sessions were done, and she closed the case. The love was real though, because she gave me her cell phone number and told me I could call whenever I needed to. Dr. Floyd introduced me to "venting" and saved me from myself. I was free.

God's Chess Moves

The case was closed and my mom couldn't move out of Gwinnett County fast enough, because their welfare office, DFCS, and the whole system had pissed her off for the last time. We moved to Sandy Springs, and so did Rashieta, so I was happy. I was in my sophomore year in high school, and I was better than ever. I was at the top of my game, taking AP classes, I was cute, and I had one of the most popular boys as my boyfriend. I was athletic, and killing it in track and field. I was social and I was friends with everyone, since I was in all level classes. I was back living with Rashieta, even though, most of my stuff was still at my mom's house. But, we lived, literally, a street apart. I just went back and forth enough to satisfy my mom. As soon as I was old enough to work, I got my first jobs at Arby's and Target. Yes, I was 16 with 2 jobs. I started at a new Arby's, and they opened a Target across the shopping plaza; so, I worked at both until I got sick of Arby's. It was so messed up, though, because as soon as I quit Arby's, Target cut my hours to like 5 hours a week; and I wasn't willing to ride the train for 5 hours, so I quit Target, too. But, I was persistent, and always had a job. I went to the mall and Rashieta got me hired at Bakers, and then, I went across the street from the mall and got a second job as a hostess at Houlihan's restaurant. I worked and ran track, and kept great grades. It came natural. I was working, but I wasn't sweating too bad, because I had money to do whatever I wanted. I was grown, and no one could really tell me I wasn't. My sister's only rule was that I go to school. I had my own space, and I was the shit and I didn't take no shit. I was an honest individual and anybody that had pressure could get it. I was good in every other aspect, but I was still angry and I would hit first. I didn't like to feel taken advantage of and I always felt like I had to stand my ground. It was a new school, and although I was sick of changing schools and meeting new friends, I liked my new friends.

By the time my senior year started, I was lit. I was living life by my own rules, I had my own money and I did what I wanted. I had just got my settlement from getting hit by a car in New York, so I was balling. I had stopped running track because I was busy, and it wasn't a priority. I had 3 jobs by this point, and was working hard to get myself a car and be fly. I paid a little bills here and there, and paid my own phone bill. I was smart, but I was over school, so my senior year I opted out of all my AP classes. I was tired of doing massive amounts of school work. I was in FBLA, so that got me my first legit job working for a credit union as a teller. On the side, I still worked in the mall and various restaurants (I would quit jobs often), including Waffle House. I was a hustler, and life was moving fast. All I knew was "get money." School became less and less important. I was dating older guys, and the guys in my high school, too, so whatever I didn't have, they made up for. I wasn't having sex with everybody, but I was using everyone for something. Whatever void I needed filled, there was someone for it.

God was more prevalent in my life than ever, and I didn't even know Him like that, yet. It was like everyone he placed in my life my senior year was so essential to getting me to that next step, and they were all working together and didn't even know each other. It started with Waffle House. When I applied to there, it was just for the morning shift on the weekends. I would go in at 6 A.M. and be done by 2 P.M. My manager at Waffle House was God sent, and I believe nothing less. He grew to know me, and made it his mission to make sure I reached my full potential. Now, I didn't know this man outside of Waffle House, but he saw something in me that I didn't see in myself. I was just hustling, and making shit happen for myself, and that's all I ever knew. I give myself credit; I didn't struggle as much with my emotions at this time, because I kept myself engulfed and busy, but I was still a hot head. I had so many jobs because I was quick to curse you out and quit. I didn't take nobody shit and I was liable to swing. I was confident in my ignorance, and that's all I knew. I even quit Waffle House after Rashieta cursed the staff out for me, and I walked out. My manager, Steve, let me come back to work 2 months later, but I think that's when he made it his life long mission to make me great. Steve came to know my sister pretty well, which eventually translated into him knowing and understanding me better. I remember the day he asked me, "What college do you want to go to?" I said, "I'm not going to college. College for what?" He was shocked by my answer, and I was clueless as to why he was asking me such a silly question like that. Nobody in my family had ever even graduated high school, let alone, go to college. College was just not an option, because nobody had money for that, and I was already working 3 jobs. So, my plan was to just keep working. Steve insisted that I had to go to college, and didn't let it go like I thought he would. In my mind, our conversation would be a distance memory, and I would just keep working and he would forget. I have never been more wrong. He brought that shit up everyday. Even when I wasn't at work, he was checking in.

Now, on the other end of the spectrum, I was in a class called, JGG (Jobs for Georgia Graduates), with one of the few black teachers in my school at the time, Mr. Taylor. JGG was a senior course that helped us transition out of high school and into the workforce. Mr. Taylor taught us life skills to be great, and how to get a job and survive in the real world. Keyword... JOB...So when he asked me about college, I was, again, completely thrown off. I answered him just the same, "I'm not going to college. College for what?" He told me the story of how he could have went to Princeton, and I won't lie, I was intrigued, because I could relate to Mr. Taylor because we were both from Harlem. I didn't know much about college, but I knew black kids really wasn't going to Princeton. Mr. Taylor took it a step further and told me I should apply to Princeton, and every other ivy league school, for that matter. He insisted that I, at least, apply, because he called it "a waste of brain." He always told me that I was smart. He would ask me, "Who do you think you are not?"

I never could really answer that question, because I never really saw myself as anything outside of hustling. Very much like Steve, Mr. Taylor would not let the college talk go. Then, very much to my surprise, by God's design, the universes aligned, and Mr. Taylor came in to eat at Waffle House one morning while I was at work. Of course, him and Steve knew each other distantly, and began talking about me. Now, it was a group effort operation: Shawna is going to college. I was stubborn, but they agreed to come together and pay for every college application I submitted. I was still clueless as to why they were going so hard, especially for me. I didn't want to apply to any colleges, but I can't lie, I was curious. I was curious about college because I had, honestly, never met anyone that been to college. I was, also, curious as to what they saw in me, because I damn sure didn't see it in myself. I wondered why they felt I would do so great in college. Shit, I wondered if I would even really do good in college. Nonetheless, I grew to respect these men very much, and if they were going to pay for the applications I would at least apply to say I did it, and not waste their money. When I got to school that next week, that's all I did in my JGG class. Forget the job modules, I was on the class computer doing college applications. Mr. Taylor made me sign up for the SAT test, too. At this point, I was just pacifying this never-ending conversation, so I applied to every school that he had me research.

The letters started to roll in, and I never told anybody, but I was shocked! I didn't think that highly of myself, so when I got a college acceptance letter, it touched my core, especially when I got more than one. I felt empowered and I didn't even know why. Of course, I shared the great news, and Steve encouraged Rashieta to take me to visit some of these schools. I told my mom about a few of the colleges that accepted me and she wasn't excited at all. I had just recently found out she was pregnant, so she was hormonal as hell. She said, "Where are you going to get money from to do that?" I could here the doubt in her voice. "How are you going to go anywhere, to anybody college? You can't do that with no money. You need to make sure you have a job."

In a nutshell, she was basically doubting that I would even pull it off. I was pissed because I didn't like anyone to tell me I couldn't do something. Hell, I was grown and I felt I could do anything I really put my mind to, so I didn't understand why she doubted me so much, and why my mom didn't see what these random people in my life saw. Neither here, nor there, she wasn't with the college shit, so I stopped talking about it. I was always one of those "I can show you better than I can tell you" people. I think I decided that day, I AM GOING TO COLLEGE. I was rebellious, and Steve and Mr. Taylor didn't know it, but it was the doubt in my mother's voice that fueled my new decision to go to college. I was going just to show her I can go to college and pay for it, and that's all the drive I needed. Steve and Mr. Taylor just wanted me to green light it in my mind, then they started on the HBCU agenda. I didn't even know what a HBCU was until I met those two. They made me do research and apply to the same amount of HBCU's as I did PWI's. At this point, I didn't care. I did it, and ran with it. I had a point to prove.

My mother had my little sister, Lyniah, 2 months before I graduated high school. Rashieta now worked in the strip club as a waitress, but still made it her business to take me up and down the east coast to visit schools. Our last visit was to Daytona Beach, FL for spring break. My best friend's grandmother worked at Bethune Cookman University, and she personally invited us down. She was as sweet as pie and she loved me before she even knew me, and that made me love her. She promised Rashieta that I would be in good hands. The beach sold me, and I had made up my mind, BCU was it. It was far enough to make my point, and the school was going to give me money to attend! I blew threw my little settlement in my senior year, but I worked all summer to try and save some money for college. I told my mom I decided on a school in Florida, and she honestly didn't believe me. She said okay, and effortlessly continued what she was doing. That was it; so, I didn't bring it up again. As I got closer to graduation, Rashieta was done with my antics. I was doing everything to necessarily be better, but not for the right reasons (it really just started as a point to prove). I was still a hot head and still rude. I was a fighter, too, and if I felt like you wanted these hands, I was going to give it to you. I remember when I got banned from the school bus and nearly suspended from all senior activities for jumping on this girl at the bus stop. I kept getting in trouble and I had to get a handle on my attitude. Mr. Taylor and Steve talked just as much about my attitude problem as they did college. I was young and caught up in my senior year fun and antics. My sister and I argued more frequently, and the underlying issue was that I was ungrateful. Although I had some hardships, I didn't give my sister credit where it was due, because she definitely made those hardships easier to deal with. She was always there, but I never said 'thank you,' nor, did I ever really understand her sacrifices. I was in my own little world, in my own bubble. I originally thought Rashieta was going to take me down to college, but she felt like since I was so grown and I raised myself (because this is what I told her while arguing), she was not driving me to Florida. She even said she wasn't coming to my graduation and packed up our whole apartment and planned to move to Dallas, TX. I was sad, because I did feel like my sister was washing her hands with me. She came to my graduation, despite her original feelings, but I think it was only because she knew my momma and knew she would miss it. Nobody never came to shit I did at school, especially my momma. So per usual, she missed my graduation, but my sister was there cheering me on. My mom met us at the restaurant afterward to eat. My sister left for Texas the next day, and let her apartment go. I stayed there in her empty apartment until the leasing office came and locked it up.

I worked the whole summer, and with each one of my checks, I brought something for my dorm room. My mom was still in denial the first half of the summer, but when she walked in my room and actually saw all the stuff I had brought for my dorm room, she was shocked. "So you're really going to college in Florida?" she asked. "I am," I said. She didn't know it yet, but I had been x'd her out of the game. I had gotten her social security number off of some paperwork and applied for the parent plus loan, so they could deny her and I could get the maximum financial aid. My mom didn't work, and was on disability, and still scamming, so I knew she wasn't getting approved. She had just had Lyniah, and my baby sister was fat and precious. My mom continued, "So you are really going to leave us here in Georgia by ourselves?" I simply replied, "Yup." That was my plan; because from the moment I found out she was having another baby, I knew I wasn't going to stick around and help with baby duties.

The day had come, and I started to load up my '94 Honda Accord with all the stuff for my dorm. It was the first time, probably since therapy with Dr. Floyd, that I actually seen my mother cry. As I walked in and out of the house loading up the car, I could feel her mood shift. She was shocked and sad. I was packing my car to drive down to Florida by myself in my little lemon, and the thought scared her. Hell, it scared me, too, but I didn't let her know that; I was still holding up my tough. Her friend, Sandra, was in town, and she insisted I go see her before getting on the road so she can look at my car and tell me that I had to much stuff piled in it. I felt like my mom was making up every excuse for me not to go. I could barely see out the back window, but I didn't care. We met her friend, Sandra, with her daughters at Waffle House, and they both sat and asked me if I was sure that I wanted to go? "Honestly, I've never been more sure," I replied. My mom was upset, and cried when I hugged her to leave. I was surprised, because I really didn't think my mom would care this much. Despite all of our issues, I loved my momma, and it was hard for me to see her cry. She made me cry, but it really meant a lot to me to know that she cared. But, I quickly tightened up because I didn't want her to think I couldn't handle it. I kissed Lyniah and hugged Sandra and her children. I got in the car, and started my 6 hour drive to Daytona Beach, FL by myself. I cried for, like, the first hour, but I never looked back. I enjoyed the game of chess and often could compare it to my life. I truly felt like I had the board (my life) in check. I wasn't thinking longevity, but God had the game setup for a checkmate. I just didn't know it yet.

HBCU vs College

Daytona Beach, 2008

I pulled up to LLC aka Lee Hall Dorms. I was a part of the freshmen honors program, which qualified me for the honors suite-like dorms. If the feeling didn't sink in before that I was really doing this college thing, it definitely sunk in and marinated over the 6 hour drive to Florida. Never in a million years did I think I was going to college, in a different state, AND be in the honors dorms. I already had achieved so much and didn't even really try; although, I didn't realize that just yet. I pulled up, and it was cars parked on the curb everywhere with students and their parents moving in. I was a tough cookie, but as soon I turned in and peeped the scene, I was intimidated. My car was packed to the ceiling, and I was by myself. I didn't think every student would be there with someone helping them move in. I was in my feelings a little bit, so I sat in the car for a second. I logged on to Facebook to a new group I had just joined strictly for incoming freshmen to Bethune Cookman, and updated my status: I have arrived. I got out the car and I immediately went upstairs, because I still didn't know who my roommate was. I was nervous, hoping she was chill like me. I walked in and I quickly found out I was late. She was in the room, already setting up her side with her sister and her momma. Kiesha was from West Palm Beach, and she was my first introduction to down south Haitian culture. Her mom was sweet, but spoke little English and much Creole. Her sister was West Palm Beach's finest—down to the green hair and gold teeth. Despite our obvious differences, they were welcoming and comforting; especially after her sister asked, "Where yo folks at?" I simply replied, "It's just me." Before I could even get back out of my dorm room, I was greeted by the Que Dawgs, asking if we needed help—probably looking for new freshmen to jump on early. Despite all the rumors and advice on how to avoid poachers, I accepted the help because I had a car full of heavy stuff. I quickly met the other Ques, and several upperclassmen. The dorms were separated by gender and GPA, and I had friends in all the dorms. The majority of my friends that I met on Facebook, in our freshman group, lived in Joyner hall. As you can imagine, with me running across campus to where my other friends were and where the boys were, me and my roommate drifted apart for more reasons than one. Kiesha was peculiar and so was I; so, that's where we clicked when we did hangout, because we always use to vent about the other nasty girls in the suite next to us who we shared a bathroom with. But, outside of that, that was all we had in common. She, like her sister, was West Palm Beach finest—hood Haitian to the core. I can't front though, she added to my valuable experiences my freshman year. Keisha took me home with her for Halloween weekend, and we went to the hoodest club in South Florida. It was girls dancing with tattoos the size of bread loaves across their ass. It was crazy, but quite entertaining. From the colorful cars, to the colorful hair, it allowed me the insight I needed to appreciate someone else's culture and understand their ways. Her mom cooked sticky rice for us; and her sister was the darkest girl I had ever seen with electric baby blue hair, and her car was the same color blue with 24' inch rims on it painted the same color. Her sister took us out the whole weekend. Kiesha always had some real stuff to say, and she introduced me to the hood niggas in Daytona. She was the first person to teach me that college niggas don't have no money, so don't toot your nose at all the locals. She had a few niggass she dealt with off campus, but they were a little too hood for me. But, hey, Kiesha was also the first person to take me to church off campus. It was mandatory that we went to the chapel on Wednesdays during the week, but they didn't make us go to church necessarily; they just encouraged it. The church she went to was weird, and all she did was sit and read her Bible. but I took a page out her book when my mom died a year later. Kiesha wasn't that bad, but we still drifted apart, because I just wanted to do my own thing and I was sick of living on campus.

Now, my friends that stayed on the other side of campus were usually who I was with when I wasn't in my dorm. Keisha was very bitchy, so I couldn't bring my friends back to my room. Therefore, I was always in their room, and this was a time to be alive. I remember so vividly when Obama was running in the 2008 election. We walked to the polls to vote as a class, and it was historically remarkable. November 4, 2008 Obama won, and I had never seen anything like it before. There were kids on top of the water fountain, hanging from the trees, and on top of cars in the street like it was a planned party that lasted the whole night. It was mind blowing. I was happy.

I had a few guys that I talked to, but there was one guy in particular that was persistent on me. He called and texted me "good morning," every morning and "good night," every night for, like, six months straight. I ignored him a lot, because I was in my prime. I was the only one of my friends that had a car on campus and freshmen weren't supposed to have cars. I had a few people that liked me, and I still had a friend back in Atlanta that I dealt with, so he was just a thought, but he made sure that he was on my mind every day. Despite all the good going on around me, I still hated the dorm life, and I was uncomfortable. I hated living with nasty girls and having to answer to an 11:00 P.M. curfew. I was at an HBCU in the honors dorm, but like your average teen, I was unsatisfied and ready to move off campus. Curfew and rules, in general, were cramping my style.

My manager turned mentor, Steve, had gotten me to college, but it was his conversations that kept me there. I needed the motivation, because I didn't want to be in college, and I wanted to just go home and work. I told him that I wanted to move off campus after my first semester; and when December came, I was standing outside the library, crying, because I was home sick (surprisingly, because I was so ready to leave my mom before) and I just wanted to go home. I didn't have a job, and the little bit of money that I came to college with was gone. I was barely getting by because soap, deodorant, and food, in general, was expensive. I was in college, but I wasn't getting care packages like my friends.

Many of my friends came from homes where their parents paid out of pocket for their tuition and took very good care of them. I was just a struggling 18-year-old in college. I felt as though my family didn't care that I was out trying to better myself, and they made me feel the wrath. I didn't have a job but I still looked for an apartment as I aggressively look for a job, as well. Every now and then, I would catch a break and go home with a friend or two somewhere in between West Palm Beach with my Haitian roommate or to Jacksonville with my fun friends. Their parents would feed us, and just make sure that we had a good time. It was then that I realized that the people around me had a luxury that I didn't have. There were days where I wish I had parents or just someone that cared to support me to be better and greater in life. I know God had a crazy plan for me, because he just made sure I always had it, even when I really didn't have it; and I could thank my friends for that.

I tried a little bit of everything my freshman year. I joined a modeling troupe on campus, but that was too demanding and catty. I eventually found new friends, because unfortunately, we fell out because I just wasn't into things there were into. For lack of better terms, they were thotting and getting turned out; and I don't like the connotation of "oh, that's your friend? Well I know how you get down." I hated that, and I eventually stopped going places with them, but, also, because I met other friends. I found that some girls came to college and got loose because they had never been anywhere, and had never been out of their parent's supervision. I felt like I have been grown for awhile, so a lot of stuff didn't impress me. Remember that boy that was so persistent, but wasn't my boyfriend? Well, I had met some friends of his friends that were girls, and we became close friends. There were all kinds of red flags as to what type of guy I was dealing with, but I was intrigued by the attention, and I often ignored the great guy because he was busy and productive and wasn't giving me the attention that I so eagerly seeked. He was older, he was charming, and he was also my access to getting off-campus. So, again, I entertained him, and I actually started to like him more than I should have. God shows you things in the beginning; it's just that our mind over matter kicks in, and you think that your subconscious doesn't really weigh as much as reality...but it does.

So, it was spring semester of my freshman year, and I found a roommate that wanted to move off campus with me. She was a friend from New Orleans, and we had life figured out. We had a two bedroom apartment with no furniture. The only thing we had was our beds, but it was fun; until I came home one day, and she was moving out. This wasn't the first time reality had smacked me in the face. When the truth did come out, she was pregnant, and the boy wasn't really accepting of it, so she couldn't afford the rent anymore. Now, mind you, I got my refund check from the semester, so I chose to save my money and pay my rent up; but, I had to find another roommate or pay the whole rent to stay in the apartment. I had grown-up problems; and not enough money to solve them. Needless to say, I didn't find a roommate that wanted to move in, so I moved out with another friend of mine from Chicago. It was a nice apartment, so I was excited. I felt like I was upgrading, again. She had parents that were very supportive of her, so they were supportive of me, too; and I appreciated it. I remember one time we stayed in Florida for the summer, and her mom flew me up to Chicago for a week just to hang and see Chicago for the first time. I had a great time; and I ate so good. Her mom was so accepting of me. She was the epitome of a mother, and that was refreshing. Like, I truly didn't have to be a grown-up with her, and again, it allowed me to understand my friend a little bit better, as well as, her culture and her dynamic growing up and why she did and didn't do some things. There were times like this that I did miss my mom, or at least mom things. We lived together about two years, but we quickly fell apart because she wasn't as clean as I was (I was OCD). We weren't best friends, but we were friends, and she had other friends that never really grew on me; I was just very peculiar about people being in my space. This is where my anti-roommate mentality developed. Every time I came home, there were people in my living room or the dishes were never clean. All the dishes in the house were dirty...every fork, spoon, knife, cup was in the sink, and this was happening daily. It didn't matter how much I cleaned up, or how many chores I did, it was still like my house was never clean enough. I remember her parents coming in town and they would clean the entire house. Then, it clicked that she didn't clean at home, so she felt like she was an adult and she could clean when she wants, and this was just the way she was raised and I had to accept that without anger. But, let's not take away from the fact that it was hard as fuck. Our disagreements outweighed our agreements and our interests were at opposite ends of the equator. I eventually made up my mind to move. I had a new crew of friends that were more like me, and my neighbor downstairs was actually friends with my new friends, so it was like we were all connected in this universe. My new boyfriend's best friend was dating my friend, and that's how we all started to hang out. I fit right in, because we instantly noticed each other's style and personality. It was a match made in Heaven. It was like, anytime I went to meet up with my boyfriend, I could see my friends, too, so it was always like a two-for-one special. I had another friend from Atlanta, and we hung out a lot, too. She still lived on campus, but I soon came to be her way off of campus and party. I had another friend, that I went to high school with, that came down from Atlanta, but she didn't come back after the spring semester because her grandmother passed away. My roommate situation just wasn't working, and I was banking on her coming back; but, I understood, and I deeply sympathized with her. My life was crumbling and I didn't really know how to deal. I called Dr. Floyd, because I had always kept her close. Anytime I felt my emotions getting out of control, I would call her and vent. She was so happy that I had made it to college. She actually was the first person to send me a care package, along with some really nice monogram towels as a gift.

I had all these new friends and a boyfriend. I had a whole new life, in a whole new state, but on the inside, I was bleeding heavy and it was eating at me every day.

I wanted to quit, and I was very uncomfortable. I felt like college wasn't for me; but, my HBCU had a unique and divine way of supporting and reminding me that I could, and I would, do whatever I set my mind to. I didn't really quite understand it then, but my HBCU uplifted me and formed me during one of the darkest times of my life.

You're Not Strong Enough...Yet

Daytona Beach, 2009

My Nana died first. It caught everyone off guard, but it was no surprise. She was older, and she had been living in a nursing home with alzheimer's until my aunt took her out to "save money." Unfortunately, my aunt did not have good intentions of taking care of her. I personally think that she died of neglect. My aunt still worked a full-time job and she just left my Nana in the house until she died. I know that my mom took it hard, but I wasn't there to really see how she was handling losing her mom. I was very insensitive to that matter. I mean, for God's sake, she was my nana! I was hurt and I was selfish, but it never dawned on me that she was more hurt than me because that was her mom. Especially since my aunt was trifling as fuck. We all knew how she died; and the even more fucked up part is, she used all of the insurance money. There was no money left to bury her, even though my grandmother retired from JP Morgan & Chase bank after working there for 25 years. The hospital morgue in New York called my mom and said that they were going to go throw my Nana's body into a potter's field if someone didn't come and claim her from the morgue. They can only keep bodies for up to 30 days. This was a shock to all of us, because we just knew my aunt had handled it, especially since she didn't call to say she had passed away! She was now a ghost along with her other 3 siblings. My nana had five kids, and only my mom showed up to the hospital to bury my nana like a decent human being. I was hurting, too, because I loved my nana and I couldn't believe she went out like no one loved her—still sitting and rotting in a morgue. My mom was sick, she had always been sick, because

she had a lung disease called sarcoidosis but this time wasn't like the rest. Nonetheless, my mom went to New York and buried her mom the proper way.

My mom called to tell me it was done, but I was insulted she didn't tell me she got a casket and buried her in a cemetery. I thought we would, at least, have a small ceremony as a family. I was so angry that my mom didn't invite me home to bury my nana. I was rude and disrespectful, because I wanted to have closure for myself. Again, never did it dawn on me that my mom was having a hard time with the whole circumstance herself, and planning a funeral was just a bit much for her heart to handle. I didn't understand that she was hurting; and she didn't have enough energy or money to have me fly home for a ceremony. She barely buried her mom herself, so it was hard for her to bring me home from college, bring Rashieta from Texas, and have our baby sister there (who was only one years old). I was so hurt and angry that I just wanted to tell her how sad I was, and that I wanted to be there. My mom didn't even get a chance to tell me that she was sick, and that she needed surgery. I hung up in her face, and she didn't call me back to argue. This was the last time we spoke. The next call I got was from Rashieta telling me that my mom had surgery, and, that it didn't go well and she was in a coma. I received the information, but I didn't digest it. There was a haze over me, and although these things were happening, I didn't want to accept it. So, I didn't want to go home, because that would have meant it was real.

It wasn't until I was casually sitting with my friends at the park that I realized how deep and serious everything was when I said it out loud. My boyfriend's roommate asked how I was doing, and I replied, "She's in a coma." That's all I said, and that's all I needed to say . I felt like the world stopped and everything and everyone was looking at me. My friend commented first. "How are you still sitting here?"

My other friend asked, "How are you not crying?" The truth of the matter is that, I didn't have the answers to any of their questions. It was like I was having an out of body experience, and I was denying everything I was seeing and hearing. I didn't want to accept the truth; so, therefore, I lived as if it wasn't happening. But, it was happening, and I was dying. We left the park that day and my friends and boyfriend asked me if I wanted to go home. I think they all put together a little bit of money to send me home, and my boyfriend gave me the rest to buy a plane ticket. All of my professors excused me from class, and my school prayed for me as I went home. I traveled home to New York, nervous, confused, and sad, as I expected the worst.

Eyes Open on You

Rashieta picked me up from the airport. We went straight to the hospital were my mom was being held. I was confused with a plethora of emotions. The only thing that distracted my mind enough from what was happening was Lyniah. She was one, and walking, and the life of the party. When we arrived to the hospital, Lyniah was the gleam of light in the waiting room. She couldn't go into ICU where my mother was being held, but I think she made everyone's day a little brighter in the waiting room. She had her stroller and her baby doll, and you couldn't tell her she was a baby herself. It was refreshing for a split second, but then, my mom's friend came and got Lyniah and ordered me to go see my mom. I was hesitating and stalling by playing and sitting with Lyniah. I didn't want to face the truth, even though I had made the trip all the way up to New York.

I walked into my mom's room, and I felt my soul shed a tear out of my eye. There were machines and wires everywhere, and her eyes were closed . She already looked like she was dead; and I felt like shit. She laid there so lifeless and unresponsive. I was scared to move around her or even get close. The doctor suggested I lean in and talk to her because she may hear me. My mom's best friend went on the other opposite side from me and said, "Shawanny made it, Dreanie." By this time, I was crying; and I couldn't stop. My feelings were just so hurt, because I was such a horrible daughter, and now we were here. I grabbed her hand and the only words I could get out were, "I'm sorry."

My last memory was me hanging up in her face; and although we had our differences, I would never want to see my mom go. I was mean every chance I got, because I just felt like she deserved it for not being there for me and protecting me when I was younger. The shit I was mad about seemed so small and didn't even matter any more. I just wanted her to know I didn't mean it, and I always loved her dearly. I was such a bitch, and all I wanted to do was tell her that I was sorry. As my thoughts raced uncontrollably, and I held her hand, she woke up. Her eyes opened and she was looking at me. Kenya screamed, "Hey Dreanie!" I was shocked. The room and everything stopped. She looked at me with so much love in her eyes, but I could tell she was fighting hard. I knew, she knew, she wasn't good. My eyes said, "I'm sorry," and all I could do was hold her. The doctor stepped in, and Rashieta was now standing right behind me. He started checking all her vitals, and he let us know that she was weak, but we could talk to her for a few. We sat and talked to her about Lyniah and promised her that she would be fine. We put chapstick on her lips. She eventually drifted back out, and my whole head was in a trance. The doctor came in and started talking to my sister and Kenya, and I was listening to him diagnose how bad it really was. I was in school for biology, so I knew what he was saying; and I knew it was bad. My mom had battled sarcoidosis most of her life, but she knew about the "if-y" surgery for a while. Her immune system was weak and wasn't building back her T-cell count. Her organ systems were failing. They had already had brought her back to life twice. The doctor expressed his opinion to let it go if it came about again. Then in a roundabout way, he went into how she may be okay with a long recovery, but may have to be moved because, of course, my mom didn't have insurance, and she had already been in the hospital a few weeks. He danced around the topic and left it short, but I caught that bullshit, too. I sat quietly in the background comprehending and digesting everything. I felt like I took 20 blows to the face. I was numb and in pain all in the same breath.

We stayed in New York a few more days in Harlem at Shaquana's house, but Rashieta had to go to Atlanta to handle my mother's business. Everyone thought it was best if I went back to school, too. We left New York with love, and Rashieta drove me back to Florida with her fiance. I got to my apartment and went straight in my room. I didn't really feel like fucking with my roommate. I sat on the edge of my bed and exhaled. I was happy to be back in my space, especially because I needed a little moment to myself. As I undressed, my phone began to ring. It was Rashieta. I hadn't been home an hour yet, and she had just left, so I didn't understand why she was calling me so soon. I answered, and Rashieta conferenced me in with the hospital. The doctor began to explain that my mom was having more than one organ system failure. They tried 3 times to resuscitate her but, he her body would not function properly with 2 major organ systems failed. He spoke all this gibberish to basically end with, her fight was over. There was nothing more they could do. Me being the hot head I am, I immediately interrupted him. "Are you sure y'all did everything? Can you bring her back and put her on the machines and we decide later? Can y'all at least try a fourth time?" I snapped.

His dry, monotone voice, again, explained the various organ system failures, and that life support wouldn't be able to sustain such a large task. I was over it. I told them I had to go, and my sister said she would call me back. I called my boyfriend and told him my mom had just died. He didn't have many words for me. His reaction was, "Wow. Damn," but, he didn't say much else. Hell, I didn't know what I wanted him to say anyway. I started to call a few other friends, but it was late so I didn't get many answers. Rashieta called me back and asked if I was okay, and I said no, and told her we could talk in the morning. I laid there and cried all night. I didn't think I could hurt this bad all over again after my grandma. My heart physically hurt, and it hurt worse than before. I didn't think I would be so upset, because I didn't always have the best relationship with my mom, but none of that shit mattered. My soul hurt, and I felt like a piece of me died all over again x10.

I went to my work study job on campus and told them about my mother. They prayed with me and handled my teachers for me. It was hard to console me and none of my friends really knew what to say. I had one friend that had lost her mom, and even she knew how hard it was to console me. She didn't say much, but

I appreciate her because she just held me and let me cry. It was an unspoken I love you and I'm sorry. I went back up to New York and everything was a blur. My sister and my mom's friend, Sandra, did all the funeral plans. That was a whole other type of stress, because we had zero dollars toward the funeral. My mom definitely didn't have life insurance. There was so much that went into a funeral, because even after my mom's friend agreed to let us borrow the money for the funeral and casket, which, mind you, was well into the thousands just by itself, Sandra wanted her money back. So, my sister promised to repay her in the near future. We were responsible for getting her casket sharp, which was probably on the list of the hardest shit I ever did in my life. My sister and I hit the streets and we went to a variety of stores looking for a suit or something nice for my mom to be buried in. Her skin and body swelled a little bit, so we had to find something nice that was big enough to fit. My sister made all the hard decisions, I was just the second opinion.

When it was all said and done we put together the cheapest, most respectable funeral in less than a week. The funeral was all the way in Brooklyn at this busy funeral home. There was no program, just a prayer card with my mom's name and birthdate on one side, and a rose on the other. No picture, no program, no tombstone, hell, it was barely any family there. My mom had 3 friends and 3 daughters. If I could count everyone that was there, I would say it was a good 15 people.. My father's mother and sister came, but none of my mother's siblings came, nor did any other family and friends. It was very small and intimate. I barely could move when it was time to walk up to view the body one last time. My cry was so silent, but it hurt so bad. I refused to go up, but of course, my mother's friend made me. I was like a zombie, and I just did what i was told. The funeral was a quick 30 minutes, and then, they were pushing us out to accommodate the next funeral. We drove to the cemetery to lower the body; and as cliche as it may seem, the sky was crying with me as it rained the entire time. My mom's friend read my mom's favorite poem that her brother wrote, and they lowered her in the ground next to her mother. It was set in stone and at that exact moment, it felt more real than ever. My mother and nana were both dead, in less than a year, and buried right next to each other.

All of my family and friends suggested I take the rest of the semester off, but honestly, routine helped. I felt I needed school to distract me from grieving. Rashieta packed up Lyniah, per my mom's last request, and that was now our baby. We drove from New York to Atlanta to close out everything there. My mom had a car, an apartment, and a bunch of stuff. The lights were off, so we had to cut the lights on to clean out the apartment. My mom received disability and every other benefit you could think of, too. Rashieta was overwhelmed with handling it all, so, although, we could have gotten a lot more assistance with our baby sister, we let it all go. Everything was a blur, and I think we were all anxious to get back to what we considered normal. We closed out everything and my sister asked me one last time if I wanted to sit the semester out, but I just wanted to get back to my normal, too, so she drove me back to school.

Pressure Busts Pipes...
& Makes Diamonds

Daytona Beach, 2010

Numb. It was late in the night when we got to my apartment in Daytona. My sister didn't stay long because her fiance had come along to help drive. I didn't feel anything, but the one thing that did bring me a thread of joy, was being in my own room, in my own space to sulk in peace. I opened up my computer and found my playlist, and just laid and cried. I was crying because nightmares were reality, and this happened, but life must go on. I was still alive and breathing, contrary to how beat up and bruised I felt. I eventually fell asleep and I woke up back in college. I started going back to class, but I wasn't really there. I actually started going to class less and partying a lot more. I would be at the beach when I was supposed to be at class; and, this was everyday. But, when I did show up, I was barely there. I was eating, but not enough, and it showed. My work study supervisors noticed, first, that I was a size 0. I was small, and was just floating, existing through life. I didn't care about nothing. I stopped going to the library and I stopped doing homework, which, mind you, I was a biology major, so it didn't take long for my grades to start slipping. I was consumed in everything, but grief. I was coping the best way I knew, which was not sober and care-free. I woke up drinking and smoking, and I went to sleep drinking and smoking. My roommate and I eventually moved into a one bedroom apartment, and it was peaceful. I did enough to maintain, but I was a mess. All I did was work, drink, and party. I still had relationships with friends and my actual professors that wanted to help me, but I really wasn't trying to be helped. I was a mess, depressed, and soaking it up with fillers. I was still chasing boys, too...anything to make me feel good.

On Tuesdays and Thursday I had a 940 communications class, and per usual, this Tuesday, like many others, I was hungover. I had already decided I wasn't going to class because I had woke up, like, 3 times to throw up. After that last throw up, I got back in bed and finally checked my phone. I had a few missed calls from my sister, and a voicemail from her, too. I started to listen to the voicemail with my eyes still closed because the room was still spinning and I heard her voice. She sounded stressed and like she was crying. "Shawana I was assaulted and I'm being arrested. I need you to come get Lyniah. No matter what, keep doing what you are doing and stay in school. Don't you ever get out your car to fight anyone. Don't let people take you there. Keep doing good," she said, before the message ended. I instantly woke up. Hell, I almost even sobered up instantly. I ran the message back to make sure I heard it right. I played it 3 times. I immediately started calling everyone I knew in Texas, starting with my sister's fiancé. He had taken Lyniah to my sister's friend's house, but he had very few details outside of the fact that Rashieta was in jail and wasn't getting a bond until she sees a judge. I called her friend, Shelly, and she confirmed she picked up Lyniah; but, she also quickly reminded me that she can't keep her long and my sister was in real trouble, so if I needed her to, she would give my sister to the state. HELL NO! I coulda jumped through the damn phone. I didn't have a plan, but I told her I would be there. I hung up and called Rashieta's other friend, JB, at this point, because I still hadn't gotten the details on what the fuck was happening. He immediately answered, and confirmed shit was bad. Rashieta was looking at a felony; and she wasn't getting out in a timely fashion. He explained that he was talking to her on her way to the gas station around 2 A.M to get some water and blunts. She had her windows down and a white guy was blocking the street. She honked her horn and he threw a large drink and his fast food wrappers at her windshield. He proceeded to yell out the window, "Shut the fuck up, nigger."

Rashieta instantly got mad and started arguing with the man. JB told me she had been going through a lot with her fiance, and just getting adjusted to having a one year old and losing our mom. So, it didn't take much to push her over the edge. They argued some more and, he said, my sister attempted to go around him. The white man put his car back in drive and drove full force into my sister's vehicle, t-boning and pinning her car against the gate. Rashieta called the cops, and then her friends. They heard through the phone when the cops showed up. Rashieta got out of the car, but they immediately went and spoke to the white man, first. As the man was telling his hillbilly version of what happened, my sister got angry and was crying, trying to interject every chance she got to tell what really happened. The officer told my sister to shut up. They exchanged a few more words and my sister was the one under arrest for assault with a deadly weapon. The cop said her car (which was still pinned against the gate) was the deadly weapon, and he arrested her. The white man drove off and went home. At this point, I was up, and I just wanted to talk to my sister, now. She eventually called a few hours later, and told me to start making my way to Texas and to try and find a lawyer. She was in disbelief that things could go this bad, this fast; but, it was happening. She told me to call everyone I could to get her out. That was the last time we spoke for about 2 weeks.

After calling around and talking to everyone, I wasn't hungover anymore, and I definitely needed a drink and then some. I went to my boyfriend's house and met up with my friends and his friends. We all sat on the couch as I told them what was happening. I asked what they thought about me bringing my sister to college and they said, "Do what you gotta do. We got you." I had been waiting for Rashieta to call me back, but she never did. I eventually starting calling and trying to find out when she would get another call, but they messed up and told me she was in the medical ward, then said, "That's all we can tell you." CLICK. I think I literally lost my mind. It eventually came back, but only for, like, 2 hours.

I called the jail back to back, demanding information, cursing people out, and getting the voicemail. They barely answered the phone. I eventually called my mentor and told him what was happening. I called everyone I could. Then I got my refund check and went straight to Texas. It was right on time, again, because my sister's friend, Shelly, was back on my line talking that temporary foster care bullshit, because I was 19 and in college. I knew how the system worked, so I knew if I let Lyniah go, I wouldn't get her back, nor, see her again. I finally made it to Texas, and I had to sober all the way up, because there was a lot to be done. I went to visit Rashieta as soon as I landed. Shelly took me, even though, I started not to like her, because I felt like she was trying to ship my baby sister off, and because she wasn't very supportive to Rashieta. She felt like having a friend in jail wasn't a good look, and she hadn't visited my sister until I came in town. Besides the fact, we went, and it was horrible. I had never seen my sister so broken; she was like a superhero to me. Her weave was gone, she had tears in her eyes as I looked through the glass, and we cried together. I felt like I was in jail. We got past the tears and got straight to business, because we didn't have a lot of time. Her rent was past due, and she was being evicted so I needed to pack up her apartment. I also needed to pack all of Lyniah's stuff and pay the lawyer. She had already lost her job, and her brand new car was totaled out in the junkyard. She was stripped of everything she had, physically and mentally. She explained that she also had been on anxiety medicine, because she went to the doctor and they diagnosed her as depressed. She had been taking the medicine, but when she got arrested, she was off her meds and had high anxiety and had a panic attack. That's how she wound up in the medical ward. Our time was up. We cried some more, and it felt like I was walking on glass walking out of the jail without my sister. We left, and got Lyniah from Shelly's family's house. She, then, dropped me off to my sister's apartment to start packing. Her fiance and her friend, JB, came to help me box up everything, but most of the stuff was from my mom's apartment in Atlanta.

It hurt, and it was way too soon, but I had to let it all go. I threw the majority of it away. I could only take so much on the plane, and the little clothes and toys Lyniah had were priority. I felt like somebody died all over again, and now I was picking up the pieces...again.

I got Rashieta's apartment packed up, but most of it was trash, because we were just taking what we could to a friend's house, so storage was limited. I packed up what I could for Lyniah, and we made our way to the airport, back to college. I coulda stayed longer, but I knew, at least, I could get back to my apartment and think straight. Lyniah was 2 years old, and not potty trained. I knew she needed her own plane ticket, but I still wanted to try to see if I could sneak her on the plane, because I was trying to save my last little bit of refund check to buy some food for my house and pull-ups for her. I got to TSA, and they turned me away to the ticket desk to show her birth certificate. I was pissed, I had brought a one way to Orlando, but they weren't letting Lyniah pass as a lap baby, even though I was holding her heavy ass the whole time! They asked for her information, and there were only two options...miss my flight or spend 400 dollars and buy Lyniah a seat next to me. I was sick. I, maybe, had $450, and I had to buy the ticket for $400 and check her luggage. As we walked back to TSA, every ounce of me wanted to cry, but I had a 2 year old who I had to keep it together for. She was just as happy as could be, and was even happier when I put her down to walk. I had no idea where we were about to get money for food and just shit, in general. I swallowed the enormous knots in my throat and we made our way to Florida. I felt horrible that I couldn't do more for my sister in jail, but I felt that I had the other half of the battle, because, at least, I had Lyniah. This was Lyniah's first plane ride, and she was excited. She didn't sleep one bit, so we played and watched movies the whole way. We landed in Florida safe and sound and made our way to my apartment. I threw her toys and little clothes down to unpack. She didn't have many clothes that fit, so I left most of the clothes in Texas and only took what she could wear. We ate at Denny's for dinner, and just let it all set in. My fridge was empty; the only thing in my freezer was liquor, and the fridge had the chaser. No food, because I barely ate, and I worked in a restaurant, so most of the time, I ate at work. I had a small apartment that wasn't baby proof at all, but I let her have her way for the first night, and I just laid on the couch and let it sink in. I had already told most of everyone that Lyniah was coming, and I guess, they would meet her the next day, because I was taking her ass to school with me.

We slept and held each other tight that first night. I loved Lyniah; and shit, I needed her at this point in my life more than she needed me. Lyniah made me feel strong, even when I felt my weakest and most vulnerable to my life's issues. Although I had no answers or solutions, I still had an ounce of confidence left. We went to school the next day, and the love was unbelievable. I would have never imagined so many people were willing to help me. I was overwhelmed with love. I didn't even know people showed that much love to individuals just cause. I felt like God was in and on every single person to work in my favor. I went to work study, and they instantly loved her. They sat me down and said, "You are going to finish school. That's it. What do you need?" I was confused, depressed, and wanted to cry all at one time. A part of me was thinking, Why do you want to help me? But, the other part was thinking, Fuck school. I need a second job. School is the furthest thing from my mind. Then my mind went to my sister, who was still in jail. My eyes filled up with tears; I couldn't help it.

"Shawana, you are a child of God, and you are wildcat. You will be fine. What do you need?" they all patiently waiting for me to answer.

I started with food. They already knew what type of life I was living, so they said that's already done. "What else do you need?" they asked. I went on. I needed clothes, because nothing fit and it was hot in Florida. I needed pull-ups and panties, because she's not potty trained.

"That's it?" they asked.

I went on. "Well I don't know what to do with her, either," I admitted. "So, I guess she needs a school; but I have no papers or records for her. All I have is my mom's death certificate and her birth certificate."

They kept Lyniah that day, and told me to go to class. I left work study still confused, because I felt God's presence, but I didn't recognize it as that, at first. I went on with my day and Lyniah stayed there until about 5 P.M. Ms. Thompson showed up to my house around 6:30 P.M. This lady was my freshman seminar teacher in the education building, but furthermore, she was an angel. She showed up with two garbage bags filled with clothes, panties, socks, undershirts (and made sure to tell me to make sure I "put an undershirt on this baby...It don't matter if we're in Florida."), shoes, toys, books, and groceries. She sat and went down the list of baby basics. "Don't be skipping steps like socks and undershirts," she said. She went on to say she had signed Lyniah up for daycare, the one attached to her church. She said everything was set up. "You just need to go up there tomorrow and fill out the paperwork. I paid the first two months," she told me. Lastly, she said that her friend was a judge, so she was going over to her house later that week to get an emergency custody petition signed for me so that I could legally have Lyniah. I was lost for words. I didn't know what to say, but I found at least a 'thank you.' I was shocked. I was shocked at how fast God could move, even though I still wasn't acknowledging Him. I was still shocked that people were moving to help me. She left, and Lyniah was joyful. She immediately starting picking out the toys and clothes she liked and wanted to try on. I was so overwhelmed with joy, as well, but the love didn't stop there.

Jagged Edged Diamond

I took Lyniah to school the next day. My mentor back at home called everyone he knew with kids to send Lyniah clothes and shoes. At the time, I was working at Ruby Tuesday's, and my boyfriend and his roommates took turns babysitting while I was at work. I even remember the day I went to work and Lyniah broke my boyfriend's friend's TV. She was in the room watching TV, and threw something at it. The TV was sitting on top of shoeboxes, and it fell. They were pissed, but they didn't ask me for any money. I was so grateful, because I knew I didn't have it, but they all looked out for me. Lyniah was like their little sister, and we were all family. Ms. Thompson got me that emergency custody petition and I officially became Lyniah's guardian. My uncle and all my family from New York were sending any money that they had to pay for Rashieta's lawyer and court expenses. Rashieta was in Texas, still trying to pick up the pieces while Lyniah and I were rolling with the punches. Despite how agitated I was about all the details and circumstances that were happening in my life, I knew there was an ulterior motive. My friends were now family, and everyone embraced this child that seemed to have just fell out of the sky. Sometimes, even more than me. Lyniah started calling me "Mommy," instead of "Wannie," and I didn't know how to take that. It was very awkward, sometimes, explaining that I didn't have a kid, and that she was my little sister that was just living with me. I would pick Lyniah up from school, and other kids would be like, "Lyniah your mom is here!" And, she would come running full of excitement. I would often tell her, "I'm not your mommy. I'm Wannie," but, that went into one ear and out the other. I think it was a comfort thing for Lyniah, and no matter how many times I told her that I wasn't her mother, she still called me

Mommy. It took me a couple months of hanging around with my friend, who just had a baby, to really understand that Lyniah was grieving in her own way and just needed to fill the void. She needed someone to call Mommy, and she need someone to willingly respond. I received it, and I put my own feelings aside. We started going to church, again, since I hadn't been to church since my mom was laying in a hospital in New York in a coma.

Lyniah and I we're finding our way in the world, and Rashieta was finally out of jail, but her situation was far from over. I got Lyniah christened, because I felt like this beautiful baby needed to be dedicated to the Lord, because the Lord was taking care of her. I felt like the Lord was stepping in to pause my unhealthy grieving, and gave me a purpose. I was declining in school, and I had every reason to want to drop out, but God made it very clear that I needed to finish strong. He positioned every person in my life to help me, and everyone who wasn't helping me dwindled away. He positioned every person in my life to give me the underlying messages that I needed to finish school and that nothing was going to stop me. There was no problem that was too big for Him; and Lord knows, I felt like I had all the problems in the world. The crazy part is, every problem that I was faced with turned out to be a bigger blessing. The weeks passed, and of course, my request to change shifts with my friends' shifts so that they were able to get and watch Lyniah, was denied. This one day, in particular, I had to call in to my job at Ruby Tuesday's because I didn't have anyone to watch Lyniah, because it was the weekend. We had just got a new manager, and she didn't care about my problems or my complicated life. She told me not to worry about coming back at all. She fired me. I was devastated, because I knew this was my only source of money, and that I was not going to be able to take care of a child now. Yet, again, I was confused and feeling crazy. I doubted God's underlying plan, because I just didn't understand. But, what I kept losing, steady turned out to be the biggest blessing in my life at the time, because I was able to file for unemployment, and they approved it. I knew about unemployment, but I never thought in a million years that I could get it. Not only did I get it, but they approved me for up to a year. I was able to focus on school and get a handle on it, while being a parent for a whole year! On top of that, Rashieta's friend, Shaquana, called just to check on me, and said she wanted to help in anyway she can. She asked me for my address and sent me a stack of blank checks, already pre-signed with the note attached: These are just to help with food and whatever you and Lyniah need. Don't OD (no crazy amounts), and I Love You, Shawna.

Shaquana was heaven sent, as well, because outside of her sending me blank checks, she was one of the few who genuinely checked on me from time to time and told me she loved me and was proud. I didn't know what to do; I just knew that God was working in my life. I almost felt like my mom had her hand in the pot, as well.

I embraced the time off. I had never been a college student and not had to work. It felt weird. I envied the other students that had parents that supported them through college, because I always had to work. It was such a luxury, and I loved coming home after school. This is where my next hobby came about, which really wasn't a hobby, because I felt like I always had the gene in me to cook. I knew I had taken on this role as a parent, so I was wholeheartedly trying to do better. I started looking at recipes and cooking the things that I like to eat. It was definitely trial and error for me, and took me a couple of times to get the rice right. But, I made everything and Lyniah loved it. She was definitely a healthy eater. We even, eventually, graduated to desserts. My little, one bedroom apartment turned into a child's dream, and we were rocking it out. I cooked almost every day, to the point it became second nature for me, but not really, because my mom was an amazing cook. I just had to nurse my hidden talent.

When all the dust settled, of course, the only one left standing was me. My friends were all living their college lives, and my boyfriend was in between wanting to be my boyfriend and taking a break. Everyone was still in and out of my life, but I had one friend who really walked with me daily in my parenting transition. Her name is Kameesha. Her daughter was one year younger than Lyniah, but they were meant to be best friends. Their first name rhymed; Lyniah and Roniyah, and they had the exact same middle name...Skye. It was freaky weird, but it was divine. They played and grew together before they even could put together letters to make words. They played so well together, and it honestly gave me and my friend a much needed break, because they would literally play until they fell asleep. It also made Roniyah more independent, because she wanted to run behind and be just like Lyniah. Kameesha also helped with my patience when it came to potty training, because she naturally had a nurturing spirit, so she always knew how to calmly talk to Lyniah and ask her what she wanted, even down to peeing in the toilet. I cooked, and my bestie did the hair. She would come over for dinner and braid Lyniah's hair. It was a well oiled machine. We started hosting our own shindigs at the house, and our friends would come over and the babies would play in the other room. We had it all figured out, and before you knew it, I was a real, full-time single mother in school.

Lyniah and I eventually grew out of my one-bedroom apartment, and I sought out a two bedroom apartment. I finally put my foot back in the water, too, and I started looking for a job. I did what I was doing so effortlessly, I barely realized anybody else noticed, but they did. I was invited as a special honorary guest to the UNCF HBCU scholarship luncheon with the mayor in Orlando. I was asked to speak about my experience at my HBCU, and how those scholarships help me, and just how far I've made it. I was shocked that they even asked me, and I was nervous. From what I heard, I realized these people already knew a lot about me, so that made me really nervous. I had never talked about losing my mom or being the first to go to college or any of the above, and it was hard to especially talk about it in a room full of strangers. Again, God's plan was far greater than anything I could've imagined. I took a stand and began to tell the audience about myself, and I couldn't help my voice from cracking. I was trying so hard not to cry, but that was like asking Lyniah not to call me Mommy; it just didn't happen. The room gave me a standing ovation, and the love was overwhelming. The love didn't stop there, though. A week after moving in to my brand new apartment—that was empty, by the way—I received a call from a woman who was at the luncheon. She had introduced herself to me after I finished speaking. She was a big executive for AT&T, and when we met, she told me that she would get together some donations; however, I didn't really put much value into what she said. I went back to school and carried on like nothing happened, but she kept her word, and she called me and she had the whole company behind her wanting to help me. It was crazy to me. I had never experienced love like this before. She was so genuine and generous. She was originally from Miami and worked in Tampa, however, she made sure there was a truck to bring me everything I needed for my brand new apartment and Lyniah's brand new room. She said she loved what I was doing, and she had a daughter at a young age, so she understood what it was like to struggle as a single mom. She said if I just kept on going and was persistent at what I was doing, that I would be successful. "Anything I can do to help you be successful, I'm going to do that. Because you are a walking blessing to this child and you deserve to be blessed," she told me. I was still in awe, but it really didn't hit me until that 14 foot truck pulled up, full of stuff for my apartment. These people who knew nothing of me, yet, furnished Lyniah's whole room from the bed to the decorations. The gave her sheets and pillows, more clothes, and more gift cards. It was unheard of, for me, that blessings could come like this.

Lyniah was flourishing, and Rashieta was getting back on her feet. She was out of jail, but she had to shake and move a little bit, because she had lost everything. She didn't have much, so I decided to keep Lyniah. We were doing far better than I could have imagined. I was entering into my senior year, and I was settled as a single mom in Daytona Beach, FL.

Love or No Love...
I'll take it

Daytona Beach 2011

Naturally, I was just rolling with the punches my senior year. I was immensely consumed in my own personal life, from my family to my academics, to the point, I didn't really evaluate my relationship with my boyfriend. I still had the same boyfriend since freshman year. In my head, he was my boyfriend, and in his head, we were on break, so he wasn't really in a relationship. He was caring, and he helped with the Lyniah abundantly, but he was a natural womanizer. When I initially met him as a freshman, he was very persistent and pursued me relentlessly. He gave me all the attention I wanted and then some. I eventually started to feed in, and he had me. I started to like him, and it was just a bad cycle of on and off after that. I spent the summer in college, and that's how we got even closer. After that first summer, he carried on as he was single, carelessly entertaining girls around campus; even some I knew. He had sex with anyone willing to give it him. It was embarrassing, yet, I still forgave him every time. I was in love, and I felt like that was all that mattered, so I kept dealing with the bullshit. Even though, every chance he got to be an asshole, he did it. We made it all the way to my senior year with the on and off thing. I remember one night, in particular, we were on, but it was a big house party on campus and all of our friends were going. All of my friends were in relationships, so it wasn't a big deal when we all showed up and my friends greeted their boyfriends. As you can imagine, my boyfriend was ugly as ever towards me. He barely wanted to speak to me, because he was still telling many people that he didn't have a girlfriend, so he didn't want me there. Neither here, nor there, he was very rude to me, and dismissed me with humiliation in front of my friends and their boyfriends. I was the only one whose boyfriend wasn't happy to see her, and he showed it. He showed his ass and went back in the house party with the strippers, and I stayed in the car with my girls. I wanted to react, but on the inside I was already embarrassed enough. We got past that, and he was over my house every day. He had an apartment with his roommates, but their lease eventually expired, so he was over my house a lot more, rent free. I paid all the bills, and I thought nothing of it because I had a daughter, and it was my apartment, so I never asked him for any money. It all happened so fast and smooth, because it just started with one overnight bag, and gradually resulted in him moving in, and us living together. Even with living and growing together, he still presented several red flags. I ignored every one of them, because honestly, he was a distraction from my personal life. At the time he moved in, my uncle that molested me as a child and was in jail for life, started contacting me . I really hadn't spoken about the incident since my counseling days in high school with Dr. Floyd, so it was very emotional and painful for me. It was like those memories were buried, and he dug them up by wanting to contact me and apologize. It really messed with me; and he was there to comfort me, so yet, again, I ignored my better judgment.

Progressing through my senior year, I decided I wanted to pledge Delta, and I went out and actually made the line. I was quickly dismissed, because I didn't make it past initiation set, and I didn't understand why, because I had one of the best recommendations that I could get on campus. I later found out that it was because my boyfriend was having sex with one of the girls that was pledging us. I confronted him and we argued, but he laughed about it. This infuriated me. I was drinking out of a glass at that moment, and I threw it at him. It broke on his head and I cut my finger. We were both bleeding, and instantly, I was remorseful. Again, we moved past this dysfunctionality, and still planned to move to Atlanta together after graduation. It was like the red flags were popping up every .5 miles along the journey, yet, I was still on the damn road.

Graduation was here, and I felt like every person that knew me personally, whether it be a teacher, my mentor, Steve, my sister, Rashieta, my best friend, Kameesha, and all my other girls, told me not to move to Atlanta with my boyfriend. Everyone felt like I should start life with me and Lyniah, alone; and if we still decided to be together, then it would be. But, they felt like I shouldn't leave college with baggage. In my mind, it wasn't baggage. I felt like we were going to get married and we were going to be together. He was supportive of me in my hardest times in life, so I felt like I owed it to him to at least give our relationship a chance. Besides that, I truly did love this person, so I felt that despite all the opinions and red flags, I would still go forward with my relationship and transition to Atlanta. It was May, and I already had a job in Atlanta, and was signed up for graduate school. My boyfriend, on the other hand, was just coming to Atlanta because I was coming to Atlanta, and he was just going to get a job when he got there. Graduation came and went. We packed up everything, and found a nice apartment in downtown Atlanta. A week after being in Atlanta, I went to the dealership and also brought a brand new car—zero miles, fresh off the lot. I was set up, and Lyniah was already enrolled in pre-K. We were doing good; however, it was not as easy for my boyfriend to get a job. As the months passed, he became very frustrated with the process, because finding a job was proving to be difficult, and the job that he was applying for, was not seeking him as a candidate. He was very stubborn and unmotivated, which turned into him not really putting much effort into looking for a job. We only had one car, which was my car, so my mentor, Steve, helped out and let us borrow his car because he had two. I let my boyfriend drive my brand new car, and I drove Steve's car so that we could both get around. I was working and going to Georgia State University, and my boyfriend was looking for a job; but, he still took Lyniah to school every morning. Most days, I came home and he was just playing a video game, and when he wasn't playing a video game, he was just being mean. Our two family household, with only one income, eventually caused a strain on our finances. All of my family and friends that were helping me with Lyniah knew I was in Atlanta, but they also knew that I was living with my boyfriend, so as you can imagine it was very hard for me to call and ask for money for bills. No one really wanted to send me money because they felt like I was living with a man, and he should be able to help out. I was honest, and I came to him and communicated with him that we did not have enough money for bills. I suggested that he call his family and friends and possibly asked to borrow some money so that we wouldn't be short on our rent and bills. He immediately refused the suggestion, because he was very stubborn and didn't want to ask anyone for help. Even my mentor, Steve, who was letting us borrow his car did everything to help my boyfriend get a job and make money. He brought him suits, he got him interviews, and even encouraged him to network with some of his friend. He even had a job for him as a firefighter, and he refused to go meet the guy. My boyfriend also refused to meet friends, get out of the house, or do anything fun. I could've easily noticed that he was depressed, but I just thought he would get a job and everything would get better.

Time went on, and things went from bad to worse. My boyfriend hated that I wanted to do more than teaching, and was working on a new business venture for a hair app. We argued every time I had a meeting or conference call about it. I felt like he didn't want me to grow or make more money, even though we were really struggling. He also hated that I would sometimes stay after school to finish my work for classes. In my mind, I felt like it would get better, so I just tried to accommodate and be considerate towards his feelings. I started to bring my work home to finish and just be around him. I even thought that if I was home more, and I cooked, he would be more happy. I thought if I went and bought new undergarments, and was a little bit more sexy, he would be happy. Nothing worked; and I became more and more unhappy, because I was putting 110% into making our relationship work. It started with very small incidents, like when I would bring my school work home, he would take his laptop and say that I couldn't use it. Even on the nights when I had deadlines, he would still fight me about doing homework at home and that I wasn't spending time with him, or I wasn't paying him any mind even though we were in the same house. Rashieta came in town for one weekend to pick up Lyniah up for the summer. We hung out and went to the spa and, had a really great weekend. I spent the night at the spa with my sister, and that caused a really big argument the next day. My boyfriend even began arguing with my sister. They went back and forth, and he started throwing all of my clothes down the steps. He put me out, even though I paid all the bills! My sister threatened me and said she would not bring Lyniah back if I didn't fix this situation, because it wasn't healthy. She left that night still cursing my boyfriend out.

I think that was the straw that broke the camel's back, because things went from worse, to as bad as they could get. He became malicious, and it started with emotional abuse. I did everything to make him happy, because I could tell that he wasn't; but, nothing helped. I remember cooking one day in the kitchen after coming home from a long day and being very tired, but I was still trying to rush and make him food, because that's what I thought a good woman should do. I was frying fish, and I burned myself really bad. He stood there and watched me cry out in pain and never asked if I was okay. He actually just went and sat down and continued to rush me, because he was ready to eat. This bothered me a lot, because now I was starting to see that he really didn't care about me, and he was engulfed in his own emotion and depression. Another night, I had ordered pizza on my way home from school and everyone ate except me, because I was pushing the deadline, like always, on my schoolwork. He deliberately waited until I was ready to eat, and took my pizza and fed it to the dog. I was tired and I was more tired of arguing. He saw nothing wrong with this behavior, and he increased his efforts to emotionally break me more and more every day. The next day we argued some more, and he locked me in our patio room for hours. I sat, and I cried, and I prayed; I knew I was reaching my breaking point. I almost climbed out the window, but I was too scared of hurting and scratching myself on the thorn bushes outside the window, and I just knew that he would let me out .... eventually. Nothing I did was good enough, and I found myself seeking answers by calling his mother and his grandmother to see if they could give me any good advice. I called his grandmother after he left me in the room for hours and her advice was so simple, yet, it cut like knives. She said, "You need to do what you need to do, baby. And, if you're unhappy, leave." I already knew everything she was telling me, yet, I was still so upset, and it hurt. The truth hurt. I found myself, a few days after my conversation with his grandmother, in the bathroom, on the floor, crying and praying on my knees with my head on the toilet, because I just wanted God to really give me a sign to show me that this was not it for me. I wanted him to really make it clear that I should leave, and that this wasn't going to be what I thought it was going to be. I cried and I was sad. I knew deep down I needed to leave because I was suffering, but, yet again, I felt like I owed it to him to at least try a little bit harder and give my all for this relationship. I felt like he was still helping me out with Lyniah. He was taking her to school everyday, and he was such a great influence in her life, so a part of me just wanted to do it for her, but on the inside, I was crying and I was very unhappy.

After my last plea to God in the bathroom, my best friend from Florida had moved in town with her boyfriend, and they wanted to get out and see the city. My boyfriend was still in a very ugly mood, however, I thought having company and familiar faces in town would help ease over our problems. Yet again, I was willing and ready to put everything behind us, and just have a good weekend with our college friends. We had planned on going out on a double date, but of course, my boyfriend didn't want to go; he just wanted to sit in the house and sulk . Originally, I felt bad, because I didn't want to leave him in the house since he was so sad, but, then again, I didn't feel bad, because I was giving him options. I was even given him another male to hang around with, and even ditch me if he wanted to, but none of that was good enough. He left me, my best friend, and her boyfriend sitting in the living room, and he went upstairs and closed the door. I sat there and finally decided that I was going to go out with my friends. So, I went upstairs to tell him that I was leaving and I would be back soon. When I got upstairs, he had my phone and was going through it. I instantly got angry, because here I was being extremely loyal and understanding; I just wanted to be in a relationship with someone that loves me and not looking to fight every chance he got. Of course, he found the one text on my phone from a random guy at the bookstore who I was supposed to borrow a clicker from for class. The guy text simply asking if I was still coming back downtown to Georgia State, and if I can meet him in the library so that we can exchange homework and clickers. My boyfriend felt like I was meeting him for a date, and I had been talking to him. That was the furthest thing from the truth. I truly didn't talk to anyone, and I just wanted my relationship to work. I wasn't entertaining anyone and I know I turned every nigga down that approached me, so I was insulted because I was actually really trying! Of course, we argued; and on that night, his emotional abuse escalated to physical abuse. He snapped. I tried to take my phone and leave, but he threw the phone on the other side of the bed, up against the wall, and it literally broke. As I went for my phone, he almost broke my arm trying to restrain me. I cried out for help, but we were all the way upstairs in the back room, so I knew my friend couldn't hear me easily; and in my mind, I instantly grew fearful. I knew that if I took too long, she would just leave with her boyfriend and send me a text, then there would be no one here to stop him. I was scared for my life, and I was fighting to get out of the room. My arm felt like it was broke, but it was just bruised. I was still fighting with everything I had to get out of that room. Physically, in the moment, I was fighting, but in my mind, I was just in shock, because I couldn't believe that he actually hit me. After the second or third blow, and being pushed to the ground like a feather, I knew I had to think quick. So I started screaming loud, crying, and yelling for my friend, and hoping all in the same thought that she didn't leave with her boyfriend, and she heard my cries. My prayers were answered, and she came upstairs to knock on the door . He was angry and proceeded to tell me that he didn't give a fuck about my friends. This made him even more angry. He started yelling at my best friend to get the fuck out, and told them they needed to leave. I was behind him begging her not to leave me, I just wanted him to let me out the house and leave with her. We pushed and pulled all the way down the steps, because I was just trying to rush past him or crawl under him, but he was much stronger than me. He wasn't letting that happen, and he proceeded to push them out of the house, then turned around and pushed me to the floor like a pillow in the way. I never felt so weak in my life. He locked the door, and when I looked into his eyes, I knew that things were as worse as they can get. I didn't know him anymore, and I was scared for my life. My best friend was banging on the front door, and he proceeded to grab me by my hair and wrap it around his fist. He lifted me off the ground by my hair and pinned me to the wall. My feet were dangling off the floor like a doll, and he was just holding me up by my hair. I could feel it ripping out of my scalp as I cried out for help. He look satisfied with my agony. All he kept saying was, "This is what you want, because you keep trying me!" I was crying, and I kept thinking, this is not what I want; and God, if this is your sign, I'm here and I'm seeing it 100%. My best friend was still at the door, yelling and screaming that she was calling the police. By this time, she even called my mentor, Steve, and he left his dinner date to come and try to help. My boyfriend let go of my hair, and I fell to the ground and he proceeded to kick me while on the floor. I was screaming at the top of my lungs for him stop, and trying, every chance I got, to run out the door; but he wouldn't let me out. Now, Steve was at the door, and he was just begging him to let me go. He even promised that he would let him walk away and go wherever he wants if he just let me out the house. My boyfriend opened the door and proceeded to tell Steve that he was not letting me out, and that I was not going anywhere. He told them that they needed to go home and mind their fucking business, then he closed the door and continued to drag me away from it.

We lived in an apartment, so you can imagine how loud our confrontation sounded outside of our walls. The neighbors called the police, too, so by the time the cops showed up, there were two cop cars and an ambulance outside, and they were all knocking on my door. They asked my boyfriend to step out. He opened the door very calmly, all while I'm thinking, this nigga is really crazy, and they placed handcuffs on him and placed him in the back of one of their police cars. I stepped outside, and I could immediately see the fear in my mentor and best friend's faces. I could tell they were just as shocked as I was, but I could also tell they were wondering how long this had been going on. Especially, when the cop asked me if I wanted to press charges, and I said "no." All hell broke loose, because the cop began to explain to my mentor that if I didn't press charges, they had to let him out of the cop car. And, the whole time my boyfriend was in the back of the cop car, he was yelling at me out of the window, "You know we done, right!? This shit is done! We over!" The ambulance decided to examine me, because I had a big bruise on my arm and in a few other places, with scratches throughout my body. I was bleeding, but very little. They decided that my injuries weren't enough for Fulton County to pick up the case, and that they could record my injuries, but I needed to press charges. By this time, my mentor was pissed, and my best friend could've fought me herself, because despite everything that happened, I didn't want him to go to jail, because his family wasn't there, in Atlanta, to help him. Here I was, caring too much and shit. I just finished getting dragged, and I was still being considerate. This, of course, made everyone think that this had been going on for a while, but it really hadn't. Steve sent his girlfriend over to talk to me, and by that time, my best friend had also called my sister. The cops were still out there, along with the ambulance, and my boyfriend was still in the back of the cop car. They were literally just waiting for me to greenlight the charges so they could go. I was scared, and I was sad, because I didn't want to hurt him, even though he had expressed and shown so much hurt towards me. My sister got on the phone and was already on her way to Georgia. She was pissed, and she was ready to kill him. The gun on the passenger seat was loaded. She also told me that if I didn't press charges, and if I kept dealing with this foolishness, she wasn't bringing Lyniah back to me, and she was cutting me off for being stupid. This hurt my heart more than anything, and I knew I had to do something. Needless to say, with everyone giving me the side eye, I went ahead and wrote my statement, and the cops drove off and went to process him. I asked my best friend and her boyfriend to stay with me that night. I felt so broken and empty. I got in the car with them and my best friend's boyfriend had a Bible in the car. It was our old college Bible. I opened it up to a specific verse: God won't put more on you than you can bear. All I could do was cry. He turned around and said, "Shawna you're beautiful; and everything happens for a reason." Although he wasn't my man, it was reassuring to hear this from a man that I knew was a friend and cared. My best friend agreed with what her boyfriend said, and she made it a point to make sure that I knew they loved me, and that she didn't want anything to happen to me. The situation that night really scared her. Rashieta was still on her way. Steve went home, but he assured me he would see me the next morning. I knew I had to let it go, but all I could do was cry. I knew this was the end of the road And, I knew that we wouldn't even be friends after this, and that hurt the most, because all I wanted to do was love him so he would love me back.

Broken

Atlanta 2013

I was bleeding on the inside I felt like every piece of me was broken; and that hurt more than any physical pain. I literally think I cried all night on a Saturday. On Sunday, I met with my mentor, Steve, and he proceeded to call my boyfriend's mom and dad to let them know what had happened, and the he was jail. Steve and I had breakfast, and he told me, "This has to be done. Y'all can't get back together. Change your number, and you need to move." I heard him, but I also I had finals on Monday, so I just replied, "I will handle it after school on Monday." Monday was my first final, and most of my other finals were on Tuesday and Wednesday. I wasn't prepared, but I went with the motions. Monday night, as I slept, I learned what a signature bond was. It was early in the morning like 3 or 4 A.M., and all I heard was a loud kicking at the door. I immediately sat straight up in my bed. I was still scared, so I asked best friend to spend the night with me, because I didn't want to be alone, so she was downstairs on the couch . Before I could get out the bed and rush downstairs to see what was happening, my best friend was rushing up the stairs. She looked at me and said, "He's here. Call the cops, now!"

My now ex-boyfriend had bailed himself out of jail on a signature bond, because it was his first offense, and walked all the way from jail, back to my apartment. Now, he was at the door, kicking it in. I was scared, and I didn't know what to do. He kept saying, "All I want to do is talk." But, as he saying this, he was literally kicking the hinges off the door. I was crying uncontrollably and praying that the cops would get there before he broke the door down. This was the first of many incidences where I gave up on the cops. I felt like it took them forever to come and, of course, my front door to my apartment was now on the floor and he walked straight in. He entered the apartment

and proceeded to say, "I am here to get my shit, and I just want to talk."

My best friend was standing at the top of the steps, and she told him "She can't talk; and you need to leave now! The cops are on their way and they're going to arrest you, again. Steve is on his way, too."

He went on and on about how this was his house, too, and he wasn't going anywhere. As the were going back-and-forth, I was looking out the window, hoping and praying for the cops to pull up. When I saw the first cop car I ran and told my best friend. I didn't know where he went, but he had left and started walking. They didn't find him that night, so they just had me write a statement. Now, I knew I had move. My door was completely off the hinges, and I was already a few days late on the rent. I was paranoid, and was barely sleeping because of my broken heart, but, now, I was barely sleeping because I was scared for my life. I went to the leasing office the next day and inquired about breaking my lease, or even moving into another apartment. Hell, even just fixing my door that was no longer able to lock because it was completely kicked off the hinges and laying on the floor. They offered to fix the door, but they said they couldn't do anything else for me without a court order or something validating why I needed to move. After I went to leasing office, I went to the police station to get a restraining order. Steve did show up, and he was pissed. I think everybody was a little bit scared for me at this point, because no one knew what I was going to do as far as forgiving him; and I think everybody was surprised about what my ex-boyfriend was capable of. Here I was, supposed to be taking finals, and I was at the police station getting a restraining order. Then I took it a step further and changed my number. I went to a few apartments and put in applications to move. I took the restraining order document to my current leasing office and they let me out of my lease, but they also let me know that they were going to evict me for the current balance due, so I needed to move within the next week and go to court. I knew I needed to move before the eviction hit my credit, so I took the first apartment that approved me, which, was honestly, down the street from my current apartment. It was a plus, because my best friend that had just moved to Atlanta with her boyfriend were living in the same complex. I did show up to take my finals, but I failed all of them. This resulted in me failing astronomy and getting a C in physics. I was also gearing up for the first day of work as a full-time teacher. I had just got hired at the school that I interned at, which was Grady High School.

Everything was in motion, and it was the first day of work. I was insecure, I was scared, and I was depressed, all over again, but it cut deeper for different reasons. I felt like I definitely lost; but it was a love lost, and it was up there on the list with people dying. I got up, and I put my makeup on and tried to look as normal as possible. I still had to go in there and perform, because there were so many people surprised to see that I even got the job. I was a young black girl in a predominately white and privileged high school, and I was teaching Biology. There were a few of the teachers who saw that I was a young girl just going with the motions, and I had a lot on my mind, but I had one teacher that always told me I carried it well and she made sure to remind me to enjoy my twenties as often as she could. I had another teacher who would always step in, and she was the biggest help that I could ever ask for being a first-year teacher. She had all the resources, and she was a prayer warrior. She never did dig too deep, but she knew I had a lot going on, and she would just pray over me and help me however she could.

It was the first week of school, and I had moved, change my number, put Lyniah in a different school, and I was trying to adjust. I hated that I had to change Lyniah's school, because she was five, and in one of the best schools in the county; but, I was paranoid that my ex-boyfriend would go to her school, so I just changed it altogether. I was moving fast and making decisions even faster. I was trying to act like everything was normal, but I was truly a mess and still very depressed. I only paid my rent; all my other bills and credit cards, I just let go to the wayside.

Anything that reminded me of my ex, I chucked it. I stop opening my mail, I stopped paying bills, and I knew I needed to retake the class that I failed for my master's degree, but I stopped thinking about that, as well. My heart hurt, and I didn't want anything to remind me of my failures, so I just stopped doing everything. I still had the eviction on my credit, and I never went to court about it, either. I cried daily, even at work. I was just so sad; but, life still went on, and as usual, I was rolling with the punches. The only thing I was doing more of, was going out. I had the worst sleep pattern, because I was so paranoid. I only slept when I went over to my best friend's house and sat on her couch, but in my new apartment, I didn't sleep . I was scared, and all I kept thinking about, was that he'd find my apartment and kick my door in again. We hadn't spoke since the last incident. I didn't know where he was; I just knew I didn't want him to find me. He knew I had a restraining order on him, also, so I was just hoping he wasn't crazy enough to look for me.

I was now a 23-year-old single woman living in Atlanta, trying to escape my love loss and pain. I went out every night, chasing a high and trying to act like I was living my best life, unbothered, when the truth was, I was very bothered, lonely, and depressed. I just was trying to forget the pain and was looking for love in all the wrong places. I eventually met a guy, and on the surface, it looked and felt great. He was new to Atlanta, and he filled all the voids I was looking for. He was very romantic and into me. We met, one night, after the club at the Waffle House, and he came on strong. He was in and out of Atlanta for a few weeks, so we talked on the phone day in and day out. When he was in Atlanta, he was always giving me gifts and money. He was friends with with several A-list rappers in the city, so we went out almost every night with the crew, to every club, strip club, after hours, all of the above. Me and my best friend was like celebrities, too, and we rubbed shoulders with a little of everybody. We would start in the studio, go to the club, go to the strip club and/or after hours spot. Sometimes, I went straight home to get Lyniah ready for school, and I went to work with no sleep at all. I was staying entertained and distracted at all cost. I didn't want for anything. Clothes, shoes, bills, jewelry, and anything I even looked like I needed, he gave me the money for. It even got to the point where he would show up with shoes and gifts for Lyniah. I was intrigued, and telling myself I was happy, because I was going out every night partying like I just dropped an album, and someone cared enough to want to help me. I had dispensable money, but it was all a distraction from one of the biggest heartbreaks of my life.

Me and my friend were cute, so all the real rappers and hitters were checking for us. I was engulfed with my new boyfriend, because he was doing so much for me; but I soon got too distracted, because he went from spending the night, to fully living with me with a corner full of clothes in my room. Now, I know how that sounds, but I swear, it literally was like, one night we went out to the club, and when we came back to my house, he had a change of clothes. Then, we went out another night, and he had a different set of clothes; and it happened that way until he had clothes over my house, and I was seeing him everyday. I noticed the frequency increased (flag one), but I was also oblivious, because he was putting cash in my hands for every bill I had, and still buying me clothes, shoes, and other things. Then, it escalated to him permanently transitioning to Atlanta, but was waiting on his car to be shipped down. So, of course, he started asking to hold my car (flag two). It was so slick, too, because it would start with, "When was the last time you got your oil changed?" or "Let me wash your car," and, naturally, I said yes. Then, he would just run the rest of his errands in my car. I swear, I blinked, and I had a whole new boyfriend and completely lost sight of my true goal of just being a little distracted. I'm sure you could have guessed, shit hit the fan quick. It wasn't more than 3 or 4 weeks, and we were arguing about everything. He got up in my face a few times, but I put it behind me, with another gift distraction. It was around the holidays, and I found out I was pregnant. I was devastated. I literally cried at the doctor's office for an hour. I just knew my life was too much of a mess to have a baby, especially with this nigga. He already had two kids that I always asked about, but he always seemed so unbothered. That was flag number 3, because it really bothered me that he didn't go home to visit his children more; and I used to tell him that, too. I told him that I was pregnant, and he said it was whatever I wanted to do. Well, I wanted to have an abortion, because I didn't want a baby at that time. Of course, as soon as I said that, it was instant attitude, because I didn't want to have his baby. But, in my mind, he wasn't about to trap me forever; I had already started to see the signs. I was so ashamed in the same thought, because I knew children were supposed to be a blessing, but I just couldn't commit to a lifetime with someone who was capable of hurting me the way my ex did. I saw the biggest sign when he refused to give the money for the abortion. I had good insurance, too, so, my gynecologist coded it special for my billing, and it only was $200. The same person that would put over 1000 plus dollars in my hand on any given day, said he didn't have $200, and I had to figure it out. My sisters came to visit, and stepped in as big sisters when I needed them. They made sure I went to my appointment, and took care of me afterward, and gave that nigga a time limit, because it was clear he was living with me.

So my sisters came in and took the baby out of the equation, and he had to leave. They sat and talked with me about staying focused, and how this, too, would pass. But, I was still so sad. Time passed, and, of course, it was, "I'm getting the keys to my apartment next week. I will be out your shit," he promised. My birthday came, and he was still giving me money, because he was still around. Ironic, huh? He, then, tried to check me about spending my money on shoes for my birthday, and I was just over it. Yeah, I had been out with him and his friends, in every Capricorn season party, but i still wanted to do what I wanted, because it was my birthday. Our argument escalated when I told him I didn't need him, or his money for shit. Which, was true. I did still teach biology full-time at this point, so I had money to pay my bills, and I even went and got the abortion by myself. He just made things more comfortable, and I had cash to play with. I was pissed, so I told him to get his clothes and shit, and anything he brought, and he needed to leave. I even threw the diamond earrings he had just bought me, too. Well, things went from bad to worse quickly, because he said, "Bitch, you think I am a joke?" and punched my right in my eye. I was so shocked, I think I went crazy trying to fight him back, but I eventually accepted the loss and decided the next best thing to do was run. He realized I was trying to pull away, and he was blocking the front door, so I ran out the back door. My best friend stayed in the same complex, but it was still a rather large complex. I ran all the way to her apartment in a full sprint. I got there and was banging on the door. My friend answered, and her and her boyfriend were looking at me like, what the fuck? I was bleeding from cuts on my arm and my lip, and my eye was starting to swell up. My friend called the police, and they came, but he was already gone. They wrote their statement and left. My actual birthday was the next day, and I had a black eye. Here I was, feeling like shit all over again. I felt like every time something else happened, it cut a little deeper. And, to put the icing on the cake, like, literally the next night, I had a note on my car from my ex boyfriend, who I had a restraining order against. He had been emailing and trying to contact me, but I was ignoring him. It was short and along the lines of, I still love you. My friend was around from the beginning, so she was honest, and told me I needed to dead my whole back and forth fiasco with the current nigga, and I needed to move, again, because of the old nigga. I knew I needed to stop accepting his money and just cold turkey him altogether. I was done, and I was so mad that I was back in the same situation so soon. I felt like it was a direct reflection of my poor decision making and trying to find love. All I found was another black eye, and more anxiety than ever. Here I was, a day before my 24th birthday. I was depressed, and my credit was declining, because anything that reminded me of my ex, I didn't pay it. I had met a totally new guy that was abusing me, and already trying to control me. I had just had an abortion, which I felt so guilty and ashamed of. And, now, I had to move because I was scared my ex would come kick my door in and finish me off, because I moved on and he knew where i lived now.

As I stood in the mirror applying makeup to my black eye, I could barely keep the makeup on, because I couldn't stop crying. I was stressed, and didn't understand how I had gotten this messed up with life. I finished my makeup because I decided I was still going out for dinner to enjoy my birthday. My best friend tried her best to make the best of it, but she knew my spirit was bruised, and I was sad. Drinking didn't help, no matter how much I told myself it did. As we aimlessly rode around the city on my birthday, I knew I had to start over. I didn't have a plan, but I did trust God; and that night, he told me to just let him work on me. That was the worst birthday ever. I was soul searching, but I was looking to every other individual to help me find it, except me.

The Art of Diamond Cutting

Atlanta 2014

I felt more crazy than I ever felt before. I was trying to get myself out of this horrible cycle, but I was in the hole deeper than before with someone who I shouldn't even allowed to get that close. I sat there evaluating my thoughts, and if I wasn't fucked up before, I definitely was fucked up now. Now, I had another crazy nigga to run from. I kept telling myself that I was moving, but I had no clue how I was going to do it. I had limited funds, and I messed up my credit so bad in a matter of months from all the bills I just let go of, plus the eviction. I started packing anyway. I started to claim a new place in the name of God, and I went and got boxes to show Him that I had faith in whatever process he had for me. My best friend and her boyfriend, and hell, everyone for that matter, that came to my house thought I was crazy, because I was literally packing up my whole house with anticipation of moving out when my lease ended in 2 months... with no place to go. When you walked into my house, all you saw was boxes, and I was packing a section a day, and just saying silent prayers to myself, because I knew God had me. Lyniah was really my faith. Hell, Lyniah was excited for a new house. She was claiming the new house more than me, and actually enjoyed packing, too. Lyniah was the highlight of most of my days, even when I was immensely sad or yelling at her. I was stressing over her, too, because her school was calling everyday about her acting out. Lyniah wasn't settled, and she was a product of her environment, and it showed at school. I was all over the place, and I didn't have the best parenting skills, so I was often frustrated with Lyniah, and would just yell at her like she really could understand. She would cry, because she was sensitive, and then I would be crying because I felt bad and I knew my parenting skills sucked. Then, we both would be crying. Even when we were home and I was frustrated, I would hide in the bathroom or outside the back door and cry my eyes out. Lyniah would find me and I would just let her knock until I pulled it together. Lyniah loved on me the most, when I needed it the most. I always felt like she knew I was going through something, so she always knew when to back off and give me a little space. She knew when to just go in her room and let mommy have a moment; and I loved her for that. We started looking for houses together and Lyniah made the process a little easier to trust. My best friend and her boyfriend would literally ask me everytime they came to my house, "Shawana, where you going?" and I would simply reply, "I don't know, but I'm going." I won't lie though, I was scared out of my mind, trying to find my faith, but at this point, I felt so low and defeated. What else was there left to do? I was praying everyday for forgiveness, because I still felt so bad about the abortion. I was getting emails, and I found the letter on my car from my first ex, so I was really trying to speed up this process, because I didn't want him to get bold enough to pull up on me. The recent ex was still apologizing and trying to do everything to get back up under me, including giving me money. I had gotten him out of my house, and out of my car, so I felt somewhat accomplished; but, on the other end, I still felt guilty, because I was taking his money even though I knew there was no chance. I had already made up my mind that I would never be with a man that hits me again. Emotionally, I was backing up from him, but he knew how to fuck with me. One night, we were all over my best friend's house, because, of course, he found a way to befriend her boyfriend, so he could always be around. I was so annoyed at this point, because it was like I couldn't get away from him. I chilled, because I was with my friend, and it was her house. The night went on and i was being cordial, and somehow my phone became the topic of discussion and that turned into an argument, of course. He took my phone and started threatening me and left. I was so pissed and angry, because here I was, participating in drama, again, with this nigga. I didn't even have shit in my phone to hide; it was just a stupid ass control thing at this point, and I was over it. I had recently brought a stun gun while out shopping for a gun after my restraining order against my ex was filed. I asked my best friend to go with me to get my phone, and asked if her boyfriend could watch the girls at the house. Her boyfriend decided that wasn't safe, because he already knew we fought before, so he didn't want him to start hitting me and my friend wouldn't be much help. She stayed with the kids, and her boyfriend drove me over to where he was staying with a friend, and I got out and knocked on the door.

"I just want my shit, and I'm done playing with you," I said, when he opened the door.

He came out with my phone in his hand, talking about it was disabled because he tried to put my password in incorrectly too many times. Then, he tried to charge for me, but he didn't see the stun gun in my hand. I lit his ass up. I was so sick of him thinking I was scared of his ass. I wish I had had a gun, but I think it was best for us, both, that I didn't. My best friend's boyfriend was half way out of the car about to help, but he was half in shock, too, because he didn't think i would use the stun gun.. My ex had thrown my phone, and was calling for his friend. "Get the fire! I'm about to shoot this bitch," he yelled.

His friend ran out with the gun, but he was hesitant in pointing it. All his friends knew that he was irate and physical with me, so they knew why I did it. "Shawty, you gotta go," his friend said to me. But, in all actuality, we were all friends, so I knew he wasn't shooting shit. I picked up my phone and got back in the car, all while he was pointing the gun at me. My ex was still trying to regain his strength to get up after I almost shock the life out of him. We politely drove off.

Now, you would think after almost shocking him to death, it would make him leave me alone, because I'm crazy, right? Hell no! He went harder than ever before. He showed up to my job with flowers and money. He would already be at my best friend's house when I got there. I even told this nigga I'm buying a gun and the next time I was going to shoot him because he was out of chances on the trying to fight me shit. I told him I wasn't fighting anymore, and I wasn't sorry either. "Oh fuck all that. It won't be no next time," was his reply. He was so in love with me, and I just needed to stop treating him so bad and acting like I don't want him. I wasn't ACTING! I was very verbal that I was done with him and his antics. I would be with my best friend, and he would be calling her phone. We would go to her house, and he was already there with her boyfriend. There would be times I would be begging both of them to ignore his call, just so I can get a break. He would be at their house and go to the car and bring back money and gifts. And, he always had somewhere in the limelight to go with every entertainer in Atlanta that was popping, so, then, it was hard to get my friends to ignore him, because now they were looking at me like, you talk to him for everything else...you could be nice this time too so we can go out. He was so overwhelming at times, and a whole next level of bullshit. I didn't have to answer to him, and I did just that. I answered when I felt like it, but the problem is, that I was still answering, and that's how he still had me. I had love for him, but I also was doing bad so he made life a little more convenient, cash wise. Outside of all his bullshit in his own life, he was a hustler... just the wrong type of hustler.

So, now, I had my whole house damn near packed up, and I can't lie, I was doing a little better since I shocked the hell out that nigga. Empowered a little, because I defended myself, and cause I now had a plan. I had a list of houses for rent, and I was driving everyday after school with Lyniah to look at least one house. I narrowed it down to two houses that Lyniah really liked. She was trying to calm down in school, and we were just loving on each other a lot more. I started working with this one realtor, and that's where all the problems came up. I did kind of forget that I had gotten evicted and didn't pay the rent on that apartment or any bills associated with it.

My credit score had dropped so low; just a year before, it was in the 800's. I still hadn't re-enrolled in the class that I failed, so I graduated, but I wasn't able to get my degree, because i didn't meet the gpa requirements. I was so angry with myself for letting my life spiral this much out of control, in such a short period. I was really down on myself, but Lyniah prayed with me often. I was really pushing for her. I started calling and making arrangements to pay. I had to go to the court and get a lien off of my name. I submitted my application, and paid my deposit. This was happening, I picked a house that was kind of far, but I was running from my past. I didn't want anyone to just pull up on me, so the further from downtown, the better. I was holding down my household, and feeding and parenting Lyniah check to check. So, I needed extra money for all the extra shit I was trying to do. That's when I started answering the phone for him again. I know, I know...but, I had everything in place, I just was short a lot of money. I had called everyone I could in my family, and everyone was kind of in a bind. Of course, he came through and did extra. All I had to say is what I was trying to do, and he brought me the money. He was still trying to make up, so I was happy I didn't have to do much, and he was keeping his distance... for now. I think he felt me backing up off of him forreal this time, so he was trying to pull out all the stops. Everything was paid, and it was moving day. I found a 3 bedroom house with a 2 car garage in Decatur, GA for the exact same price as my 2 bedroom apartment in Midtown. I was happy. I was really trying to hide where I was moving from my ex who was giving me the money, but he was persistent, and I was just trying to survive with me and Lyniah. Needless to say, he was the one who helped me move. Then, he came in and helped me paint, and furnished my house. I was still taking everything he was willing to give, and I still felt like I had control. I was keeping him at bay; and it was good for a hot second. He started feeling himself again, so I quickly went back to cursing his ass out and not answering the phone. I also sent all the furniture he put in my house back, because I didn't want him to feel like he had something in my house that was his. That made him mad. This nigga said, "I will pull up and crack your fucking skull." I knew he was serious, but I wasn't scared of his threats. We had been going back and forth a few days, but this day, we were arguing over the phone, and, of course, his next response was, "I'm on my way to your house." FUCK SHAWANA! If I had never been mad at myself before, I was really mad at myself, now. This is exactly why I wasn't supposed to let him know where I lived. I had Lyniah and Roniyah that morning, because I took them both so they could play and Kameesha could have a break with her boyfriend. They were in the room, up and playing already, and I was on the phone arguing and texting. He got there and wanted to talk. He rang the doorbell and came in calm. We walked to the kitchen and I immediately started off, "Don't get comfortable. You gotta go. I really don't think it's much to talk about." Here I was, being honest, again, yet, firm. I had already text my friend to tell her of his threat, and she asked if I wanted her to come over, but I never text her back. I told him that the girls were there and I couldn't talk to him at the moment, because I was angry. He asked me to step in the garage when I asked him to step outside. Once outside, he asked, "What we doing? Why you playing with me?" Again, me being honest, I simply replied, "I'm not. But, I don't want to be with you." He was really mad that I sent all the furniture back. We were talking—well, I was talking—and before I knew it, he had smacked the shit out of me. Here we go again. I was less shocked, I would say, now, because I immediately jumped on that nigga. I started scratching and punching him. My stun gun was too far away—all the weapons were too far away—so fuck it, we were fighting. I was sticking my fingers in his eyeballs, and doing everything to over power him even a little. He grabbed my car key off the hook and tried to jump in my car and drive off. So, now I'm scared as hell, thinking he was about to steal my car. I snatched the driver side door open and I started going crazy. I was punching and trying to grab his eye out the socket. Lyniah saved the day, yet, again! She opened the garage door and saw me going crazy and fighting and started crying. I looked backed, because, now, he had managed to put the car in reverse and we are rolling back as I was punching and pulling his arm and feet. I was trying to reach for the mace in my middle arm console. I started yelling at Lyniah, "Call Kameesha! Call the cops! Go... do it now, please, baby." She ran and got the house phone and called my best friend. first. My neighbors were the ones who actually called the cops, because when they looked outside, I was getting dragged as my car was moving, still fighting and holding on to this man. The lady across the street stepped outside and starting yelling, "the cops are on their way!" He got scared and got out the car and started walking. He cut through the trees and disappeared. I got in my car and pulled it back in the garage. I went in the house, and both children were crying. I sat them down and calmed them down; and the police came shortly after. I hate the police, but this officer that showed up still told me some real shit. He was mean, and straight to the point, like a father. "You gotta stop doing this and dealing with these shitty niggas," he said. He let me know there was a record attached to my name every time I called 911. He was able to look back to the first incident with my first ex. He said he saw when I called after my ex left the note on my car, and he saw when I called after that, when I had the black eye and I ran all the way to my friend's house. He knew everything, and then he went on to tell me, "You are young, pretty, and got a lot going for yourself. You are a teacher for God's sake (he already knew that. too)." He told me to get me some "one on one" time and love on myself, but leave these men alone. "Give yourself a moment to heal," he said. I was angry and tired, too. I wasn't bruised up, but I was sore as hell from fighting for my life. I was tired, at this point, but I received everything this stranger at my door was saying to me. I hated the damn cops, but he was right. I knew I had to do better. He ended with, "You will be fine, but just remember what I said."

Kameesha pulled up when we were ending, and she was pissed, naturally. I had mentally tainted our precious little girls, and I was still an emotional mess. The cop left the house, but he sat in the car awhile. She went in and checked on the girls, and then she came back to ask if I was ok. Then, she grilled me and questioning why I back peddling; because, she knew what I was trying to do, too. I made a promise that I was going to reset and get it together. I was actually going to take the cop's advice and heal, find my happy, and be at peace, because I really was a wreck. I was getting my shit together, financially, but I was outdone with these niggas. My ex was still threatening me via text message, but I ignored him, and continued to make him feel bad about disrespecting me in front of my daughter. I told him if he pulled up on me unannounced again, I was shooting, first, and calling the cops next. He was very apologetic, but I was done with the shit. And, I meant it this time. I didn't want his money or anything else from him. I decided I didn't need to date or be around anyone. I took the time to decorate my house and get into a few DIY projects. I started getting into church more and my sister, Rashieta, helped with that. She was out of jail and at peace, going to church and having faith; and I was astonished, honestly, by her own personal growth. I admired my sister so much, at this point, I just had to try it out myself. I started tuning into her church online, and actually listening. I found another little jewel in me.

Pray. Then Pray. Then Pray Some More

I was lonely as ever, but I was toughing it out. I had been watching church online everyday and every time I felt sad or lonely, I played a random sermon. I fell asleep most nights, crying and listening to sermons, but I was getting better. I was spiritually working on me, but Lyniah was declining in school. I was working and maintaining everything by myself. I was feeling better, but my baby still hadn't found her peace. She was still asking about my first ex. Her asthma and allergies were on a million, so she was constantly sick. There was a girl in school that was bullying her about her mom dying, and saying she's adopted. She was stuffing homework in her desk and not bringing it home. The school was calling me in for meetings, and I wasn't calm, because I was royally pissed with the little bully, that I wanted to fight her myself. I called and demanded a meeting with the girl's parents and the administration. That led into a conversation about Lyniah doing poorly in class. They said that they thought she needed to be in remedial classes and may need to repeat 2nd grade. They recommended I take her to see a doctor to help her focus. We went toe for toe, and I started sitting in on Lyniah's classes twice a week, because they claimed that she was the problme, and that she was acting out and couldn't read. I knew Lyniah could read and write very well, so I wasn't taking anything laying down. I was emailing all the head district people about the negligence of the school; telling them how they were casually handling the continuous bullying ,down to them labeling my child based on their lack of classroom management and differentiation skills. I went in; and I didn't care that they knew my boss, or that I worked down the street. I really didn't care, because they had been playing me from jump, with the school choice as a teacher, because I was the young, black girl, and they forced my hand with placing her in that school. Lyniah hated going to school, and I didn't blame her. She often told me she heard the teachers talking about her and how she's failing. She felt like they were standing around calling her stupid, and the kids would overhear and tease her about her grades. When I observed her teachers, I could tell Lyniah was scared to raise her hand and ask any questions, because the teacher was a maniac. She was always yelling, and the kids were bad as hell, just to get her to react. I saw it the first day. Every time my baby put her hand up, she put it down; and she would just sit there. I knew Lyniah had it in her, I just had to put my best foot forward with this one. She was growing up and having a real issue, and just when I thought I figured this whole parenting thing out, again, I was stuck. I started seeking resources from my coworkers and working with Lyniah on all our free time. I put her in Kumon 3 times a week for math and reading. She hated it, but I kept lecturing her on how much it would pay off and help her be her best self. She was trying, but Kumon challenged her IQ, and her confidence. It helped me help her build her confidence, too, because when she was gaining points and winning, she was so proud of herself. She was working hard, and it made her happy that I was proud of her, because I had really been hard on her for awhile. All I knew was tough love, so she got a lot of that.

My best friend moved in with me during this time, after a very similar situation with her boyfriend. I was so angry that she had to experience that same, exact pain I had experienced. These niggas were so out of line; but I was happy. I was in a better place, and able to help her find peace and be at ease with her daughter. I felt like I had gone through everything she was going through, so God wanted us to come closer, and share what I had been learning from Him. It worked, and we all made each other a little better. Lyniah and Roniyah were as happy as can be, because they shared a room and were sisters now. Kameesha moved into my office room, and we became a real family. She was the first real person to teach me how to mother a child. Not just provide, but to actually be nurturing. I never had that, and I had never really truly been pregnant to develop that, so I was clueless. She would often tell me, "Kids need hugs and kisses. They need love. You don't always have to be so serious." I was serious, because I felt like that was how you stayed focused, and I wasn't the loving type, because I didn't grow up like that. She told her baby she loved her everyday, multiple times a day; and I was in awe. I had never seen that type of mother/daughter love. I was intrigued. And, her baby, Roniyah was a lover, and she loved on me, too. She always wanted a hug randomly throughout the day, and she would come hug me. She loved that I cooked and wanted to cook with me. It was so weird, at first, but, of course, she made Lyniah want to hug me everyday and kiss me goodnight every night, and tell me she loved me. It was intoxicating .

My mentor was always a phone call away, and he was helping with anything I fell short on with Lyniah. Even if he didn't have it, he was always reaching out to his network, getting clothes and toys for Lyniah. He finally got me together with this school situation and calmed me down. I was on roll and definitely pissed the principal and whole administration off at the school. He found a private catholic school for Lyniah, 10 minutes from my house. He said they would take her mid-year, and he thought the change would be good for Lyniah. He commended me on working hard, but he also let me know I needed to focus more on Lyniah . She needed me now, more than ever, and although she enjoyed the best friend-sister family, she still needed one on one mommy time to ask me her personal questions. It didn't dawn on me until my mentor sat me down in the room, in the corner, and said, "Hey you're fucked up, yes. But, Lyniah is grieving too, and she needs you. She has questions and is confused about her feelings with all the crazy shit you're going through. You need to talk to her more." He knew I was still hanging and drinking and consumed in my own world. I was also still looking for love from guys that were only looking for sex. I wasn't getting abused anymore, but I was being used. I was angry, but Lyniah was sitting across from me, and I looked in her eyes and she confirmed everything he had said. I received everything he told, and he didn't know it, but I decided to be celibate that day; because I knew that my body, shit even my soul, needed isolation for growth. The constant disappointment from men was still affecting me. I enrolled Lyniah in private school and Kumon Saturdays became our personal lunch days. We would sit and talk about everything. She was sad about my mom, but Lyniah loved me so much, it was easy to oversight in thought. What really puzzled Lyniah, was why she didn't have a father, grandmother, cousins or anything. She wanted to know where here family was. I was so used to being whoever Lyniah wanted and needed me to when she was young. Hell, I was grandma at one point, when that's what they were learning about in daycare. Now, that she was older, she knew the difference, and knew our little family was small. She knew her mother had died, but Lyniah wanted to know about everyone else. I was honest and explained how families would grow. I would meet a king, one day, and she will have a father. That made her excited, because she really liked the idea of being a big sister and a having a real baby. These were all very far in the future in my head, but I gave her all the false hopes she needed. She was finding her peace and doing so much better in school. I was proud, and told her every chance I got, and that made her even more happy. I felt like she was happy to impress me. My mother was Catholic, so I also felt like this was sent directly from God, and this was His will, and my mom's, too.

I didn't know it in the midst of it, but God also had a will for my new job. My first day on the job was the day after I was dragged down the steps by my hair and experienced one of the most traumatic moments of my life. I couldn't take off that first day, but I wound up working there, in the same high school, for 5 years. As you can imagine, I was vested in my career, and as I grew and changed, the school moved through change as well. During that 5th year, everything changed. We got a new principal, and it felt like war was waged on me, yet, again. The new principal came with new administration; and they were sent to steal, kill, and destroy. I was still learning innovative things, but I was a pretty seasoned teacher by this point. My evaluations went from outstanding and proficient, to poor and developing. My principal insulted my intelligence and challenged my competency in biology, when it was actually her, who was wrong and ignorant. They were giving me the lowest evaluation scores I could get, because they could. It wasn't just me, though; it was many of the other faculty members, too. So, I tried not to take it personal. I knew something was happening, because they were fucking with me more, and I was about to quit. I know I felt the old Shawana bubbling to the surface, and I was about to walk right off the job. I was coaching JV cheer, and I loved the students, but the administration was unbearable.

The straw that broke the camel's back came about the first week in May, right before the semester was about to end. My evaluator walked into my classroom and explained how I would need a professional development plan (PDP) for the following school year, and I needed to sign off on my acknowledgment. Now, a PDP was like the set up to fire teachers and tarnish their teaching certificate. I politely said, "No thank you; because I quit." I packed up and called downtown to the district office to officially resign. My assistant principal, at the time, called me personally, and respectfully advised I finish the semester and close out my grades. He expressed to me how change was good and everything would be alright, because I was really a great teacher. "With change comes growth, and I see you growing and going on to do great things Ms. Brooks," he said. I finished the year off on a good note, and the assistant principal submitted all my recommendations in the highest regards.

Evolution
Atlanta, 2017

My next job was 10 minutes from my house, and my salary increased by $4,000. It was definitely a good change, but it was different. I was at an alternative credit recovery charter school, which was code for demographically challenged and bad as fuck. The kids were definitely not downtown Atlanta kids, and they had a lot going on. Change can also be so divine by design, because I felt like I ended up right where I needed to be. Many of those kids needed to meet a Ms. Brooks, and embrace the fact that everyone can learn. I was one of the lead after-school STEM teachers, and that's when we had the most fun and I saw some of their brains light up. I met so many great, young individuals, and curated some great connections that fueled my passion to mentor. I always knew I enjoyed speaking with my students outside of my science content, but I never really thought about it in a serious thought of pursuing as a alternate career. There were so many things wrong, but still some things were going right for me on a daily, and I was quite impressed with God's work at this point. I won Teacher of the Year, during my 6th year teaching biology at the worst school I had ever taught at. I was shocked, and just a little taken aback that they saw me doing my thing. I was honored and relieved, because it was proof, for me, that I was doing something right. I was coming into this whole trust thing with God, so I had the tendency to still worry.

Murphy's Law is a law because of living proof individuals like myself. "If things can go wrong, they will." I was learning to not doubt the devil, but furthermore, I was learning to not underestimate the power of your faith in what you are doing; good, bad, or indifferent. It was the first Wednesday in May, and we were having our first faculty meeting of the month. The meeting was extra crowed that day, but I squeezed in and found a seat, because mainly all the extra new people were standing. The Dekalb County school district officials were accompanying the faculty meeting along with the charter school boards of trustees. They were all there as one big family to tell us the school was closing. The district was voiding our contracts and the school was under new management effective immediately. The current administration was escorted out and under investigation for stealing money and for negligence. So, translation: you all need to find new jobs and we are not about to place y'all. Everyone would need to put in a application to the distract, and apply as a new employee. I was done listening to the bullshit, and I admit, I am a work in progress, because I got up and walked out of that meeting. I was done, and either way, the cookie crumbled, they were wrong; because, I know they knew this for a while, so why string us along until all the really good job offers are taken? It was insulting and very unprofessional. I left that meeting to go get Lyniah, and immediately created a new teacher profile in all the county portals that night. I probably put in 12 applications that night. They took over the school the last 3 weeks of school, and brought in movers to pack up the school and put everything in storage. The gave us our last checks and a severance package for all those individuals they knew were going to have a hard time finding a job. They told us to go to the actual bank and cash all of our checks, because all school activity for the charter school would be shut down June 30th, and that included all financial accounts. They were real bogus, but I was getting better at working hard under pressure. I wasn't getting too many hits off of my portal apps, and I knew it was because it was the end of the year, and all the last minute jobs didn't go up until late. I started calling the schools and emailing the principals for interviews. Of course, once I got one call back for an interview, I got 5 interviews. I had options, now.

God is keeping a record of how many times I made a comeback. I embrace the growth, and I am more aware, now, than ever, that the journey started the day I was born and is far from over. I am constantly re-evaluating how I can be better, but the process is in motion. At 28, I take pride in saying I am the mother of a 10 year old, who is amazing, beautiful, and smart. She is more confident in herself, because I am more confident in this evolution process. I have been teaching Biology for seven years, and celebrated being recognized by my HBCU, BCU Alumni as an extraordinary "40 under 40" Alumnus. I was also was able to still celebrate being "Teacher of the Year" 2017-2018. I was so humbled by such an honor, back to back, for something I do so effortlessly. Even when I would get discouraged in the good fight, God had a way of reminding me that I was on the right track. I took a step back from my entrepreneurial hair endeavors and evaluated everything. My company, iWeave International, is breaking ground right now, and the hard work is coming full circle. I started, ThatGirl! Foundation, alongside my co-founder, and created a nonprofit for "that girl just like me." I have ultimately made up my mind that I want to evolve and serve as an example, or even proof, that yes, "you can, too."

Conclusion

I am happy to see growth in myself. At 28, I have experienced a lot, but I've learned from every situation. Every chapter in the book was a defining moment in my life and of my character. The fight definitely doesn't get easier, but I've gotten stronger. I haven't had one good encounter with a man, yet, and even after all my abusers, I was still was looking for love from people who were looking for sex and convenience. I've been isolated and celibate, and I have learned to love a little deeper and a little different, with every experience, and that is truly My Agape. I have learned to love myself and understand that undying love that God has for me. I struggled to write this book, and really speak my truth, but it has been the epitome of freedom. I have met so many amazing people while writing that has inspired me everytime I stopped writing. They also inspired me to believe in myself and see all the blinding light that they saw in me. I was supposed to get laid off 2 months before I was set to publish. God set everything up for the level up. I got hired at a better school. I got a severance, so that I could finish paying for my book and pay all of my bills. I want you to know with every situation, in every chapter of this book, was God's design. He needed me to experience and learn from it. He needed me to be the light and example of His glory, and that's what I want you to take away as a reader.

Each chapter is meant to give insight to at least one individual experiencing something similar. Each chapter is meant to show you the bad, then highlight the journey back to great. God was a major part of that journey, and what's for me has alway been for me. My love for you, as a reader, is undying and that's why I chose to share this kind of love. God loved me and carried me gracefully to where I am now. I love God so much that I was obedient in sharing this testimony and sharing the love I have experienced from Him and found for myself. I am a walking example that things do get better and it's not over until you say its over. If it's tough the reward is great . The power of self love is undeniable and I finally found that. My Agape. I hope you love a little different after reading my story and find your Agape.

"For it is God who is working in you, enabling you both to desire and to workout His good purpose" Philippians 2:13

About the Author

Shawna Brooks is an educator , mentor , entrepreneur, author and mother. As a biology educator for the past 7 years, she has naturally migrated into her mentoring role and is Co-Founder of ThatGirl! Foundation, a nonprofit organization that advocates for college and career enrichment for teen girls. Shawna is also a fearless entrepreneur who is the head of operations for a major e-commerce hair company, iWeave International. In addition to her many roles, Shawna is an amazing mother to her beautiful younger sister, whom she adopted in college. As an author, Shawna uses her life's experiences and lessons to exemplify how divine purpose can prevail, and success can triumph any obstacle with the right mindset.

Connect with Author Shawna Brooks on Social Media

Instagram: @shawana_f_Brooks
Facebook: Shawana Brooks